# POOL & BILLIARDS

KNACK

# POOL &
# BILLIARDS

**Everything You Need to Know to Improve Your Game**

**Bruce Barthelette**

**Photographs by Eli Burakian**

Guilford, Connecticut
An imprint of Globe Pequot Press

Copyright © 2011 by Morris Book Publishing, LLC

Editorial Director: Cynthia Hughes
Editor: Katie Benoit
Project Editor: Tracee Williams
Cover Design: Paul Beatrice, Bret Kerr
Interior Design: Paul Beatrice
Layout: Kevin Mac
Diagrams and overlays by: Jamey Gray and Lorraine Enik
Cover Photos by Eli Burakian
Interior Photos by Eli Burakian with the exception of pages xi (bottom), 26 (right) and 45 (left): Illustration © Cugianza84 | Dreamstime.com; 120 (left): © Wikipedia Commons; 204 and 205: Courtesy of Allison Fisher, www.allisonfisher.com; 206 (right): Photo courtesy of Anne Craig; 207 (left): Copyright © R. Jeff Smith 2009; 208 and 209: Courtesy of the American Poolplayers Association (APA); 210 (left): Courtesy of Joe Carr; 210 (right): Courtesy of Ewa Laurance; 211 (left): Courtesy of J.R. Calvert, Inside POOL Magazine; 211 (right): Courtesy of Ewa Laurance; 212 and 213: Courtesy of Mike Massey; 214 and 215: Courtesy of Andy "The Magic Man" Segal

Library of Congress Cataloging-in-Publication Data

Barthelette, Bruce.
  Knack pool & billiards : everything you need to know to improve your game / Bruce Barthelette ; photographs by Eli Burakian.
    p. cm.
  Includes index.
  ISBN 978-1-59921-959-2
  1. Pool (Game) 2. Billiards. I. Title.
  GV891.B37 2010
  794.7'3--dc22
                                                                2010029313

The following manufacturers/names/logos appearing in *Knack Pool & Billiards* are trademarks:
all®; AT&T™; Brunswick®; Championship®; Cuetec™; CueTrack™; Delta-13™; ESPN®; Harlem Globetrotters®; Kasson™; LiquidWick™; Make-A-Wish Foundation®; McDermott®; Meucci™; Miller Lite®; PING_PONG®; Susan G Komen for the Cure®; YouTube™

Printed in China

10 9 8 7 6 5 4 3 2 1

*To my mother who I lost in December, 2009. I think about you every day. I would never have been able to do this without you. Thank you Dad for being the wonderful father that you are.*

## Acknowledgments

Many thanks first and foremost to my wife, Ann, who has been everything to me. She has been at my side supporting and encouraging me since the first day we met. Without her, I am sure that I would not have the successes I enjoy today. Together, we make a great team. She is the love of my life.

Thank you, Jamey Gray, the current world trick shot champion. Jamey started out playing in my local league, and, within two years of deciding to learn trick shots, he became the world champion. Jamey and I will be partners for the 2010 *World Cup of Tricks* tournament on ESPN. In addition, Jamey played a major role in helping me write this book; I can never thank him enough.

Working with Eli has been such a wonderful experience. The photos came out better than I could have ever imagined. Throughout the entire photo shoot, Eli was exceptional in his professionalism. He has a way of making everyone feel comfortable. I feel very fortunate that I was able to work with Eli on this project and hope that I get to work with him again in the future.

Thank you Nicole Netherland for all you hard work and dedication on the writing of this book. You kept me organized and focused. I would still be working on the book if not for all your hard work.

Thank you, Mike Massey, one of my closest, generous, and kindest friends. I was honored when he asked me to make a speech at his Hall of Fame induction, and it has been his encouragement and teaching that have helped get me to where I am today.

Thank you, Sal Conti, another truly great friend who has helped me with just about everything. Sal even helped me develop many of the shots I played during my first appearance on ESPN, and he continues to be a major support person in my life.

Thank you, Andy Segal, another one of my closest friends and the current most talented trick shot artist in the world. We have been partners now on ESPN for four of the past five years. I know that whenever I have a question about anything, Andy has been right there to answer it.

Larry Hubbart, I really wanted you in this book for so many reasons. I respect you for being such a gentleman who along with Terry Bell allowed me to enjoy a wonderful life doing something I love.

# CONTENTS

# INTRODUCTION

I started out playing pool when I was just four years old. I acquired an interest for the game from the first time I picked up a cue stick. I stayed with it, practicing at home on a table my dad purchased from a relative. Rarely a day went by when I didn't pick up a cue and start knocking pool balls around. Both my mother and father were wonderful in allowing me the time and support to practice the game. My older brothers, Ken and Ron, were my main opponents. It seemed like every night I would play one of them in a game of pool. It was because of all this practice that I was able to turn into a very good player.

Pool became an even bigger part of my life when I got old enough to go into pool and bar rooms. During one of these nights out with my friends, a top player in the local area—known for winning most every match—challenged me to a game. Within the hour, he quit and walked out of the bar. The joy I felt from winning a game against such a top player increased my serious interest in the sport.

While in college, I found I was better at being around a pool table than sitting in a classroom. After a slew of various jobs, I found myself drawn, once again, to my favorite pastime. One night, I was playing a money match against a local pool player. It turned out to be the luckiest night of my life. It was the night I met my future wife, Ann. While she did not play much pool to start, she knew how much I enjoyed it, so she learned the game and became a very good player. Together, the two of us joined a local pool league and started playing regular games. We enjoyed the

viii

league so much that we eventually found our true calling as APA pool league operators. Another league operator, Jon Waidlich, showed us the ropes of the job. And on March 22, 1989, the Connecticut APA pool league began operation, and we worked hard to build up our league. Since its humble beginnings, the league has expanded to over 900 teams throughout the state of Connecticut.

My job has afforded me the opportunity to meet and learn from many professional pool players, including the late, great Willie Mosconi. I've been fortunate enough to have played with and develop strong friendships with many top pros, including Mike Massey, the greatest trick shot artist ever to hold a cue. In fact, I credit Mike with introducing me to the world of trick shots. With his encouragement and teaching, I competed on both *ESPN Trick Shot Magic* and the *World Cup of Trick Shots,* and went on to a successful career as a professional trick shot artist.

## About the Book

When I was asked to write a book on the game of pool, I wanted to be sure that I would be able to put out a book that would cover all parts of the game, from basic techniques to family-friendly games to advanced trick shots. This book covers a wide variety of material, including all the skills needed for a beginner pool player to advance his game. It also houses a lot of material for the seasoned professional looking to brush up on his game.

For the beginner just starting off, you'll get tips on the best cue sticks and pool tables to buy, how to care for your equipment, and how to execute the proper grips. The book goes into great detail on how to assess the proper angle for the shot, where to hit on the cue ball, and how to play both offensively and defensively. You'll also learn the rules and

etiquette to playing such game staples as 8-Ball, 9-Ball, and Straight Pool, among others. For the more advanced player, you can entertain friends and family with trick shots of varying levels of difficulty, including Mike Massey's famous boot shot. You can also brush up your knowledge on the more obscure pool games, such as bowliards and speed pool.

Knowing that not everyone will go on to become a professional in the sport, I want to stress the family-friendly nature of pool. The sport is fun for people of all ages, from little tots to seniors. Many families have pool tables in their homes, so it's a great bonding experience for kids and parents, as well as for friends and neighbors, with a quick game

of pool, or maybe a few friendly competitions. If, by chance, you do find yourself, like I did, in love with the sport of pool and would like to turn your hobby into a career, there is also information in this book on how to get into tournament and league play and beyond.

## Pool & You

The game of pool has strongly and positively affected my life, and I encourage you to read up on the player profiles in chapter eighteen to learn more about how other professional players got to where they are today. Some of the greats are profiled in that chapter, including Andy Segal, the current top trick shot artist in the world, and Ewa Laurance

(better known as "The Striking Viking"), a former number one ranked player in the world and a member of the Billiard Congress of America Hall of Fame.

Like with any other sport, the game of pool takes dedication and practice, but it is also a lot of fun. With the advent of technology, the pool community has become global, with many international superstars leading the rankings in today's top tournaments. Also with the advent of technology and the advancement of equipment, players are creating more exciting, intricate trick shots daily, and are inventing new and crazy games all of the time.

While the history of pool is rich with unique characters and legendary stories, there's always a place for new history, a chance for you to write a chapter in the history books with your own experiences and achievements. My hope is that you come to love the sport as much as I have, and that your experiences with pool take you far.

Oh, and if you should have any questions throughout your pool journey, please feel free to drop by my Web site, brucebarthelette.com, and ask me some questions. Good luck with the book; I hope you enjoy it.

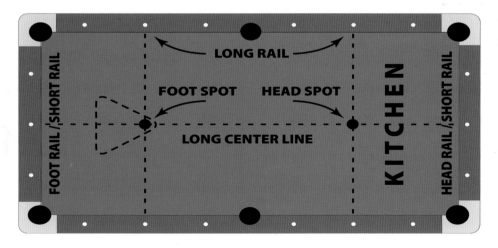

# EQUIPMENT: POOL TABLE

## The first step toward being a good pool player is getting the right table for your needs

Purchasing the right table will make the game of pool much more enjoyable. Three factors are important to keep in mind when researching tables: (1) size of the room, (2) pricing, and (3) professional installation.

The size of the room that you intend to put the table in is important. If the table is too large for the room, you will feel cramped when shooting. Ideally you want as much open space around your table as possible. Many tables are installed in basements, and support columns can get in the way. Because most of the shooting is done at the end of the table where you break the balls, you want to keep it free of any obstructions.

New pool tables with slate beds range in price from $1,000

### Table Size

- Pool tables come in three basic sizes: 7-, 8-, and 9-foot lengths. The width of a table is always half the length. Therefore, a 9-foot table is 4½ feet wide.

- A 9-foot table has a playing surface of 50 by 100 inches.

- A good minimum height for your light is 36 inches above the cloth.

- For 7- and 8-foot tables, a three-light fixture will give plenty of light. A four-light fixture is recommended for a 9-foot table.

### Slate

- The best tables have slate beds. Other materials will not hold up over time.

- Because of their weight, most 8- and 9-foot tables come with three pieces of slate.

- The gap between the spaces is sealed with a special wax (bees' wax) that makes for a level playing surface.

- Never lift a pool table that has three pieces of slate. The slates will separate, and you will need to have a professional level your table.

to $10,000 and up. The average player who wants a quality table installed in his home should expect to spend around $2,500. This gives you a great playing table that should last you a lifetime. If you want a professional tournament table, you will be looking at $6,000 or more.

Installing a pool table is much more complicated than meets the eye. A professional pool table mechanic will make sure that the cloth is stretched out properly, the table is perfectly level, the rails are tightened to proper specifications, and the table is in the best location for the space that is available.

## Drop Pockets or Ball Return

- On many tables you have the option of drop pockets or a ball return system.

- The ball return system has gullies that run under the table and allow pocketed balls to return to the racking end of the table.

- Drop pockets or a ball return system is a personal choice.

- The ball return system is priced slightly higher.

### Room Size versus Table Size

The standard cue length is 58 inches. To comfortably fit tables of these sizes into your room, be aware of these dimensions:

- 7-foot table: 13 by 16 feet

- 8-foot table: 14 by 18 feet

- Oversized 8-foot table: 14.3 by 18.5 feet

- 9-foot table: 15 by 20 feet

# STANDARD ACCESSORIES

## You will need to buy some accessories after installing your pool table

Now that you have installed your new pool table, you will need to buy a few more items. Depending on which table you have purchased, it may come with a starter package that includes a set of balls, a rack, a bridge head, chalk, and four one-piece cue sticks. This gives you everything you need to get started.

As with a pool table, you can spend different amounts of money on any of these items. The better your game gets, the better equipment you will want to play with. A large variety of pool balls, racks, and bridges is available. When you start to travel to different pool rooms and friends' houses, you will observe a wide variety of these items. This is the best way to

*Pool Balls*

*Racks*

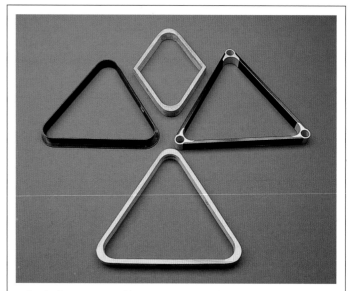

- The game of Pocket billiards uses 2¼-inch-diameter balls. A variety of different style balls is used.

- On television the cue ball has red spots on it. These help the viewer see the spin applied by the player.

- Televised games also use different-colored balls for the 4, 7, 12, and 15 balls.

- With the traditional colors, the 4, 7, and 8 balls all looked the same on television.

- Racks have come a long way from the days of the thin plastic-edged ones.

- Nowadays racks are designed to allow players to rack the balls more tightly.

- A tight rack makes for a better break and increases the breaker's chances of

- pocketing a ball. In tournament play it is essential that the balls are racked very tightly.

- With these new racks, it is much easier to produce a tight rack. Racks are usually made of wood, metal, or plastic.

find out what equipment works best for you.

You may want to get many other items as you start to play more. You will need a brush to clean your table after you are done playing. Brushing your table and keeping it clean will make playing more enjoyable. It will also keep your hands from getting chalk all over them. A tip-shaping tool will help keep you from miscuing. Keep some powder around to help if your hands start sticking. Just don't use too much powder, or else your table will look like it has snow on it.

If you play the game of 14.1 Continuous, better known as "Straight Pool," you will need to purchase a set of beads or a score counter. Some of the older pool tables have the counters built right into the rails.

You may also want to consider decorating your room with some classic pool art. You can even find the rules of pool set into a picture frame.

## Mechanical Bridge

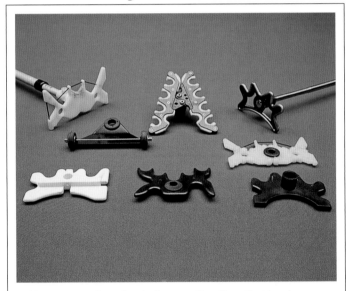

- Many types of mechanical bridges are available.

- One of the more popular bridges is called the "moose head," named for its shape.

- There is the standard bridge head, which is found on many 7-foot bar box tables.

- One item that has become popular is a cue stick extender. It is an attachment that slides onto the butt end of the cue to make the stick longer.

## Chalk

- Chalk is the dry abrasive substance that is applied to the tip of your cue.

- To chalk up properly, use the edge of the cube of chalk. Start at the middle of your tip and work to the outside.

- Apply an even coat of chalk to the entire tip.

- Never chalk your tip by placing the cube over the tip and making a circular motion. You will not get an even coating of chalk.

# ADDITIONAL ACCESSORIES
## Now that you have all of the basic equipment, here are a few more things you will need

A few years ago not many accessories were made for the game of pool. You could purchase the standard equipment only at your local pool room dealer. Nowadays the situation has changed. There is a large variety of accessories to choose from for your game room. Some of the items are new to the game, whereas others have improved from their original designs.

Recently home game rooms have become popular. More and more pool enthusiasts are adding such a room to their houses. During a get-together, this room is where everyone will want to be. Depending on your budget, the sky is the limit for what you can add to a game room. Even with a limited budget, given the vast range of accessories, both in price

*Gloves*

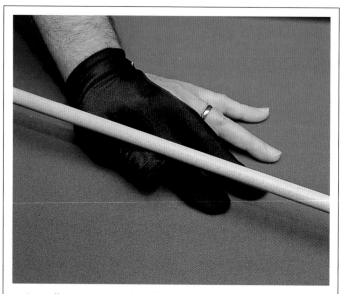

- A small percentage of pool players wear a glove. It helps them get a smooth stroke without having to use baby powder on their hands.

- The glove is worn on the bridge hand and should be a snug fit. It helps the cue slide through the fingers with little or no friction.

- If your hands perspire easily, then the glove may be right for you.

*Pool Table Cover*

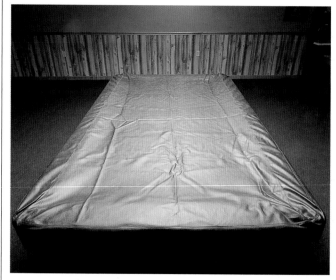

- If you spend a good deal of money on your pool table, then you need a good table cover to protect it.

- The cover will protect your cloth from dust. If you have children, it will protect it from spills and damage from toys.

- You can get creative with covers. Some turn your pool table into a dining room table, whereas others allow you to make it into a Ping-Pong table.

and type, you can still create a beautiful room.

For the player the modern pool game has become much more enjoyable with more accessories. Cue sticks, tips, bridges, cue extensions, lighting, and cloth have seen great improvements over time. With new accessories being created regularly for the game, the choice of accessories is endless.

Pool accessories can be purchased at a variety of places. You can check out the Internet or go directly to your local pool room dealer. If you are not sure of what you really want or need, it is recommended that you go to the local dealer, who will be able to answer your questions and steer you in the right direction.

## Cue Stick Holders

- One of the worst fates that can befall your cue stick is for it to fall onto the floor. There is a good chance that it will get a nick in the shaft from the fall.

- Such a nick is difficult, if not impossible, to get rid of. It will be a distraction when you shoot.

- The best way to prevent a fall is to carry a cue stick holder in your case. Such a holder will help ensure that your cue will not slide and fall to the floor.

- It is an inexpensive tool to protect your cue.

## Cue Cases

- The number of cues you take to your match or even to your friend's house for a friendly game will determine the size of the case you need. The average person has two cues: a playing cue and a breaking cue.

- Cases generally have one space for the butt end of the cue and two for the shafts. These are called "one-by-two cases."

- It is a good idea to get a case with at least enough room for two butts and four shafts.

- Cases come in a wide variety of materials, colors, and prices.

# CUE STICKS

## Your cue stick is the most important item that you will need to buy for your game

Your cue stick should feel like an extension of your body. The cue stick needs to feel comfortable in your hands in order to shoot confidently. If this is your first cue stick, it is highly recommended you go to a reputable dealer and have him help you. He will be able to answer all of your questions and point you in the direction of the perfect stick.

You can buy a stock cue at your local dealer's showroom, or you can have one made from a cue maker. Price, weight, taper, joint, type of wood, length, type of shaft, and type of wrap are just some of the decisions you will have to make.

A wide variety of cues (outlined below) is available. The one that you will use most is called a "shooting" or "playing" cue.

*One-piece Cue*

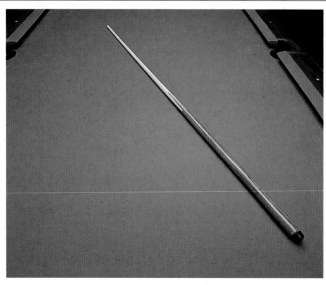

*Two-piece Cue*

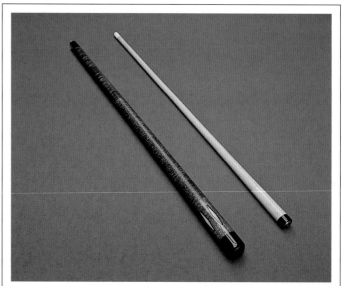

- The one-piece cue is usually used as a house stick.

- This cue is difficult to travel with, so most times it is the house stick used in pool rooms, bars, and homes.

- One-piece cues are inexpensive. It is a good idea to have some around, especially when you are having a get-together.

- Most one piece cues have a very basic design.

- The two-piece cue is the most popular among professional and better amateur players.

- With the two-piece cue, you can carry extra shafts to a tournament and not worry about popping a tip off.

- A player has a wide variety of cue choices, including in weight, design, and price.

- The two-piece cue is perfect for travel because your cue case can fit right into your suitcase.

You should buy an extra shaft for this cue. If you pop a tip off during your match, you will have a backup.

Before you put any chalk onto the tip of your new cue, check it out thoroughly to make sure that it is straight and that there is no damage to it. Roll it on a pool table to be sure it doesn't wobble. Look down the length of the cue and rotate it. By doing these tests, you should be able to tell if the stick has any imperfections.

## Break Cue

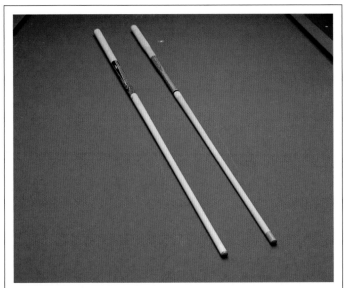

- Just about every cue manufacturer makes break cues. The tip on the break cue is hard, unlike that of the playing cue, which has a softer tip.

- A break cue usually costs less than a playing cue. It is not necessary to spend a great deal of money on it. You use it only one time per game, and that's if you have the break.

- Many players like a heavier break cue, but others break better with a lighter one.

## Jump Cues

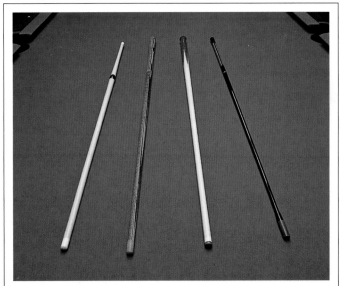

- Jump cues are about 40 inches in length, which is the minimum legal length of a cue.

- They are light and have a hard tip.

- Most manufacturers produce jump cues. These cues are designed for normal jumps, close jumps, and long jumps.

- Before shooting jump shots at a billiard room, you need to ask if it's allowed.

# CUE STICK ANATOMY
## Get to know the parts of a cue stick

Many people make cues, but only a small percentage make a great cue. George Balabushka, Gus Szamboti, and Herman Rainbow are a few of the great cue makers of the past. Because of the equipment that they had to work with, they were able to produce only a few cues per year. George Balabushka set up his workshop in his garage. His cues were in high demand by many of the top professionals of his day.

Because of modern technology, the lathes used today allow cue makers and companies that do mass production to produce more cues. More people today than ever before own their own cues. Twenty to thirty years ago it was common for players to use house cues. Only the better players, who were really dedicated to the game, owned their own stick. It is common now to see players with a playing cue, a break cue, and a jump cue. And they probably have a few more cues at home.

### Tip and Ferrule

- Almost all tips are made of leather. You can get them in soft, medium, or hard.

- Top players prefer medium to hard tips instead of softer ones for better feel and control.

- The tip should be in the shape of a dime or half moon. You don't want it to be flat or mushroomed.

- The white area below the tip is called the "ferrule." Look for cracks. If you find any, you will need to see a professional for repair.

### Joint

- The joint is the area where the two halves of the cue stick connect.

- The connecting pin is either a screw or a metal pin. All of the older cues use screws.

- Pins are now used for quick-release cues. Pins make changing shafts easier.

- You will need to know the pin and thread size if you order a spare shaft for your cue.

Consumers have so many more options in the overall design of their cue. Depending on the cue maker, you can customize every part of it. You can go as far as to put diamond inlays in it, although this will really increase the cost.

One company even has a ten-year waiting list. The company allows you to order two cues when your name comes up. It does not offer all of the options of other cue makers, but the cue is one of the best-hitting cues available.

## *Butt*

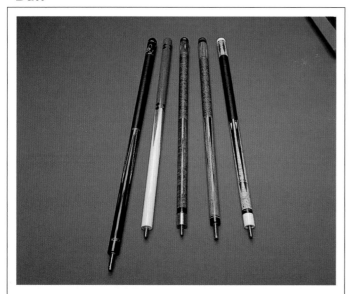

- The butt end of the cue is where most of the cost comes in.

- Cues that have inlays are much more expensive than cues that have decals.

- You can change the weight of your cue by adding a weight bolt, although not every cue has this option.

- The wrap is the section of the cue that you grip with your back hand. Irish linen is the most commonly used wrap.

## *Shaft*

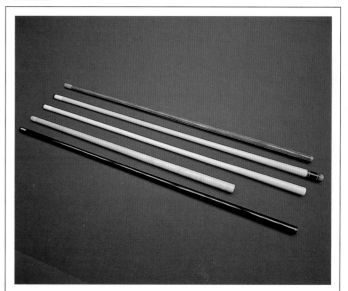

- The shaft is the section of the cue that starts at the joint and goes to the tip.

- The most common shaft has a 12- to 13-millimeter tip.

- Keep the shaft clean of chalk buildup and dirt. Many products are available. It is important that you buy the correct products when doing work on the shaft.

- The preferred material used to build a shaft is maple.

# CHOOSING A CUE

## Now that you understand more about cues, you need to know how to choose one

Nothing is better than going to a billiard trade show and checking out all the innovations. Doing so gives players a chance to talk with the dealers and ask questions.

Only a few trade shows are held each year in the billiards industry. If you are serious about purchasing a high-quality cue, these are the best places to go. Almost all of today's top cue makers have booths at these shows.

If you are unable to attend trade shows, you should be able to find a quality cue maker in your area. The best way to find one is to ask your pool-playing buddies. Word of mouth is really the best advertising a cue maker can get.

Another way is to try out your buddies' cues. When you find

*Price*

- Price is wide open. There is a variety of prices for cues. This will depend on the workmanship and cue maker.

- A cue in the $70–$200 range with a reputable name in the cue-making industry is all you need to start.

- You want a cue that will deliver a consistent hit and feels comfortable to you.

- Talking to a knowledge-able salesperson is highly recommended.

*Craftsmanship*

- Craftsmanship involves the choice of materials, amount of detail, time, and the quality of the cue maker's work.

- Materials can include exotic woods, precious stones, and a variety of other choices.

- Detail is found mostly on the butt end of the cue. It can feature inlays, points, rings, and so forth.

- The best way to determine the quality of the cue maker's work is to ask around. When it comes to the value of a cue, the maker's reputation is key.

one that you really like, you will have done the hardest part. Now you can go to your local dealer with a good idea of what you want. You will know whether you have the right cue as soon as you shoot a few balls with it. You always have the option of changing the tip and shaft if the ones that come with the cue do not feel right.

## Weight

- The weight of the cue is strictly a personal preference. The most popular weight is around 19½ ounces.

- Most playing cues weigh between 18 and 21 ounces. Break cues vary in weight depending on a player's preference.

- Jump cues do not weigh as much and can be as light as 12 ounces or less. There is no minimum weight requirement.

- Massé cues are the heaviest of all cues. They can weigh as much as 25 ounces, the maximum legal weight.

## Feel

- There are numerous ways to pick a cue. One way is to choose three to five cues that you really like and put them on a table.

- With your eyes closed, pick up each one and stroke with it. The one that feels best is the one most recommended to buy.

- You want to hit a few balls with the cue. Doing this will let you know right away if the cue feels right for you.

# CARING FOR YOUR CUE
## A good cue should last you a lifetime if you take proper care of it

Almost all cue sticks are made of wood, and because of this, you need to perform maintenance on them. The tip, depending on how much you play, can last for years. If you are the type of person who continually uses a file on the tip, you will need to change it more often.

The shaft of your cue should be kept clean. Avoid sanding it down too much, or else you could change the proper taper of the cue. It is always a good idea to keep your hands clean when you play. The stick will slide through your bridge hand easier, and you will not get chalk buildup or dirt on the shaft.

Storing the cue properly is essential for its longevity. Cues that were made in the 1950s and 1960s and maintained and stored properly are still straight and in good condition. If you are unsure of what you need to do, ask a professional. If you know a cue collector, he will also be able to show you the proper methods to maintain your cue.

### Storage

- When you are not using your cue, it should be stored in a cue case or cue rack.

- It is a good idea to spend money on a good case.

- It is never a good idea, however, to leave your cue leaning against a wall. This is most likely when your cue will get damaged.

- Properly storing your cue when it is not in use will protect your investment.

### Tip Care

- Having a tip tool with you during a tournament or league play helps to cut down on miscues.

- Leather tips need to be scuffed up so the chalk will better adhere to the surface.

- You also need to reshape the tip when it mushrooms or loses that half-moon shape.

- You need to learn the proper technique from an experienced person.

You always want to be careful where you place your cue down. If it is in a high traffic area with many people walking by, there is a good chance it will get knocked over. Another thing to be aware of is to always know where your cue is. Sometimes by accident, or on purpose, a cue stick is accidentally taken or stolen. If you are in a room full of people and you need to leave the area, have a friend watch your cues or take them with you.

## Shaft Care

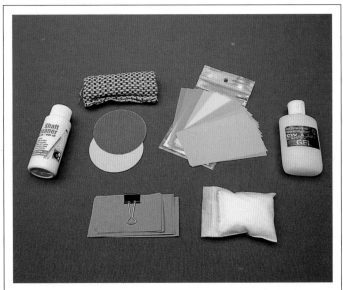

- Many players neglect proper care of the shaft.

- Chalk and dirt build up on the shaft and ferrule, affecting the smoothness of a stroke.

- It is easy to care for this part of the stick. Liquid cue cleaners remove buildup; you can also use 600-grit sandpaper.

- Only a small amount of time is needed to keep the shaft like new.

## Maintenance

- To get the best maintenance, go to professionals. They do all their work on a lathe.

- Most professionals can put on a new wrap, change a ferrule, clean the shaft, and put on a new tip.

- Most cue professionals do an outstanding job, but it's also good to get recommendations.

- Ask around and find out who does the best work in your area.

# STANCE

## Having a solid foundation and balance is essential to becoming a better player

Having good mechanics is important to continually improve your game. When you watch professional tennis players and golfers, you see that they have great technique. They address their shots the same way each time. To make shots consistently, you need to be consistent in your mechanics. If you learn bad mechanics and practice with them, your game will improve very slowly or not at all. The top players in professional sports always seek out information about their game. It is easy to learn something each time you play.

It is also a good idea to practice with different partners. Where one of your partners may be great at safeties, the other one may be great at offense. Doing this will help forge

*Feet Placement*

- Place your feet at a comfortable distance in order to achieve good balance.

- The average distance is 1½ to 2 feet apart. This distance will vary depending on your height.

- You need to find the point where you feel comfortable and completely in balance.

- If you lose your balance during a shot, you're more apt to miss.

*Stability*

- The best way to test your stance is to have a friend come over and give you a little push.

- If you lose your balance easily, then you are not in the proper position to shoot.

- You will need to start over and adjust your feet accordingly.

- As in most sports, you need a good foundation to achieve good results.

your game and make decisions on the pool table easier.

Many qualified instructors teach good mechanics. In England, where the game of Snooker is popular, players hire a coach at a young age. This is why most Snooker players have a similar stance at the table. When you learn the correct way the first time, it will help prevent you from picking up bad habits. In the United States most players are self-taught. And because of this fact, many styles of play exist. Until recently it was difficult to find someone willing to teach the correct way to play the game of pool.

Even if you learned the game at a young age, it is a good idea to continue working on mechanics. You should watch the better players' mechanics for a comparison. Working on mechanics should help you become a better player. Not only will you pocket balls, but also you will have more consistency.

## Forearm

- The forearm needs to be vertical when the tip contacts the cue ball. This stance will give you the best opportunity to make a shot.

- Keep your cue on a level plane throughout the entire stroke or for as long as possible.

- One of the biggest mistakes that amateurs and new players make is to raise the butt end of the cue stick too high. Lowering the forearm to a level plane will create better results.

## All in Line with Cue

- When you get ready to shoot, first you should step back from the table, line yourself up, and then walk into your shot.

- You want to have everything in a straight line. To confirm this, have a friend stand behind you when you are in the set position.

He can check to see if your alignment is off.

- If you are at the table, and your alignment is off, you will need to stand up and start over.

# GRIP
## Players often overlook this part of the mechanics

How you grip the cue can make a big difference in the amount of action applied to the cue ball. Only a few basic grips are used in holding a cue. After all, it is your back hand holding the butt of the cue. Not many grips are available.

On normal shots you want to grip your cue in the same place every time. Players have a tendency to move their hand forward when they are in a pressure situation. Doing this will cause you to change your normal stroke. When you do this,

making the shot and playing position will be more difficult.

Another bad habit is to twist the wrist during the shot. You want your grip to remain in the same position throughout the shot. Doing this will help to ensure a straight follow-through. If you find yourself twisting the wrist during the shot, you may want to use a wrist strap, similar to what bowlers use. This strap helps to keep your wrist straight on all of your shots.

### Where to Hold the Cue

- Your hand placement on the cue is generally about 4 to 8 inches from the end of the butt.

- This placement, of course, depends on the length of the cue, your size, and the type of shot.

- Be careful to not let your grip hand choke up too far on the stick.

- You should grip the cue in the same spot every time unless a specialty shot dictates otherwise.

### Gripping Too Tightly

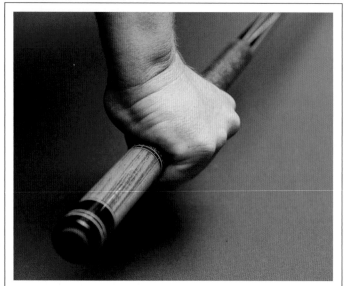

- Gripping too tightly on the cue will cause you to lose action on the cue ball. This grip is sometimes referred to as the "white knuckler."

- This type of grip will most likely happen when you are in a pressure or game-winning situation.

- Don't worry. It commonly happens to inexperienced players. You will now be better prepared the next time a situation comes up in which you feel your grip getting tighter.

The most important aspects of a grip are being comfortable and relaxed. If your grip is comfortable, then it will be easier to keep it relaxed all the way through the shot. It does no good to have your grip relaxed if just before you strike the cue ball the tension builds up and you tighten your grip. Stay in a relaxed position until you hear the ball go into the pocket.

Almost all professionals make their stroke look effortless because they are relaxed. After you are able to control this part of your game, you will quickly become a better player.

## Gripping Too Loosely

- Holding the cue too loosely is a much better problem than holding it too tightly. It is also much easier to correct.

- The danger of holding the cue too loosely is that it may slip out of your hands after you hit a shot.

- Also, your hand may move during the shot, sliding along the butt of the cue and causing you to lose some control.

## Just Right

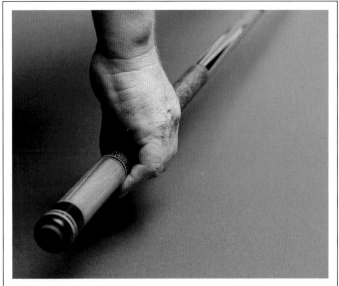

- The best way to describe the perfect grip in pool is to pretend that you have a bird in your hand; you don't want to hurt it, but you don't want it to get away.

- This will help you produce the proper tension.

- When the pressure is on, you should think back to this analogy.

- You will become a more consistent player when using the proper grip.

# BASIC HAND BRIDGES
## The bridge hand is placed on the table and is used to guide the cue stick

To advance your game to the next level, you need to have a solid foundation with your bridge hand. The shaft of the cue needs to glide through your fingers with the proper tension. You want to have enough tension to control the cue but not so much that it will not slide through smoothly.

During the course of a game, you may use three or four types of bridges. The location of the cue ball and what you attempt to do with it will be the determining factors.

Most new players start out with an open bridge in which the cue stick sits between the forefinger and thumb. Some of the best players in the game of pool have used the open bridge with great success. This bridge works well for many

### Bridge Distance

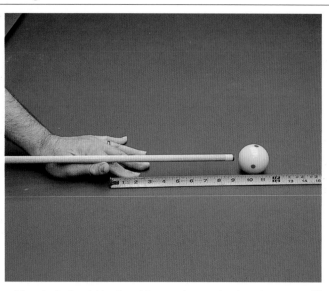

- The shaft should be 6 to 10 inches from the edge of the cue ball to the opening in your hand.

- You need to find out which distance is comfortable for you. This distance is for your standard shot.

- In certain situations you will not be allowed the luxury of this bridge, and you will need to adjust.

### Open Bridge

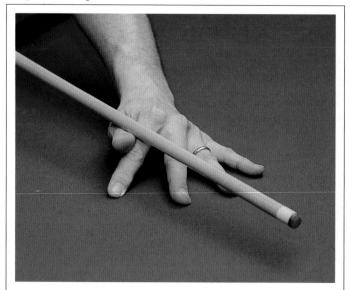

- To make an open bridge, simply place your hand on the table and let your fingers spread out.

- Arch the fingers upward a little bit. Bring your thumb over your index finger, and it will form a bridge.

- This is one of the most common and easiest bridges to make.

- Most beginners start off using an open bridge.

shots. As players progress and play the game more, they most likely adapt the closed bridge. This bridge gives more control when you aim. It also helps you keep the stick on a straight plane more easily than an open bridge will.

What always matters most is which bridge you feel most comfortable with. It is recommended that you experiment with different bridges, but don't feel you have to lock into a certain one right away. Seeing a professional use a closed or open bridge does not mean that this type of bridge is right for you. Go with the one that gives you the most confidence.

After you have mastered a good bridge, your game will improve quickly. As in many other sports, a good foundation is necessary to achieve success.

## Closed Bridge

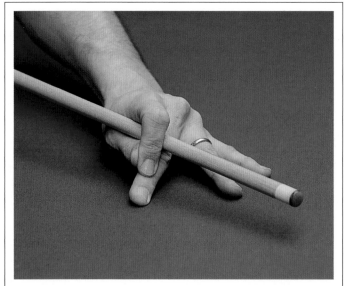

- To make a closed bridge, start by laying your hand flat on the table.

- Arch your hand back and have your thumb and index finger form a loop. The cue stick will fit nicely in the opening.

- Again, you do not want to have too much tension. It needs to be loose enough for the cue to slide through smoothly and tight enough to have control.

- The remaining three fingers will spread apart and act as a support for the entire hand.

## Bridge on the Rail

- When you shoot off the rail, you need to adjust your style of bridge.

- One way to do this is to lay your shooting hand on the rail and put your stick up against your thumb.

- Then take your index and middle fingers and bring them over the top of the stick.

- This position will give a solid foundation to execute the shot.

# ADVANCED HAND BRIDGES
## At times the conventional bridges won't work

Many scenarios occur during a game of pool. It doesn't matter if it's 8-Ball, Straight Pool, or One Pocket. The sport of pool is one in which you get to use your imagination. Players need to be creative and be able to adapt to any situation. Practicing situations in which the cue ball is in a tough spot to make contact with will go a long way in improving your game. To master these situations, you need to know which advanced technique to use.

Everything starts with the solid foundation in the bridge hand. For example, some shot setups limit your ability to use as solid a bridge as you would like. You have to be able to steady yourself as much as possible, use a specialty bridge, and concentrate even more on these shots. Your chances of missing will be much higher than with a shot that you can shoot with a normal bridge.

When you are in these positions where a specialty bridge

### Elevated over Ball

### Low Bridge

- One of the more difficult shots requires having to shoot over a ball. In most cases you will need to use an open bridge.

- Bring your hand as close as possible to the blocking ball. Keep your stick as level as possible; concentrate on a good stroke.

- Avoid using English on the cue ball unless it is absolutely necessary.

- You must stay down and give this shot your complete concentration.

- When striking very low on the cue ball, you need to lower your bridge hand a bit. You want to level out your cue as much as possible.

- You can do this by spreading out the three fingers you are using as a base. This is a very subtle adjustment.

- You do not need to lower your back hand grip to the point that it feels uncomfortable.

is needed, take extra time to set up. Go through your normal routine to boost your confidence. When you get to that confident point, it is time to take the shot. Just remember: Everyone misses at some point. You are trying to have yourself in the best position possible to achieve success.

If you attend a tournament where either professionals or top amateurs play, watch how they get out of trouble. Keep a close eye on how steady their bridge hand is. And finally, remember to be patient; it takes years of practice to master each of these bridges.

## Open Bridge on Rail

- When the cue ball is close to the rail, an open bridge works best.

- Keep plenty of space between the cue ball and your hand to allow room for your stroke.

- Try to keep your cue stick as level as possible and keep good balance. Keep your head still during the entire shot and follow through.

- Also spreading your fingers apart will help with stability.

## Elevated Bridge on Rail

- This is a difficult shot to control because you are able to hit only a small portion of the cue ball.

- Also, you are elevating the butt end of the cue. Every time you have to raise the butt end of the cue, aiming becomes more difficult.

- With the elevated open bridge, you have a difficult time controlling the shaft.

- This type of bridge is required at times and will need to be practiced.

# MECHANICAL BRIDGES

## The longer the table, the more you will need to master the mechanical bridge

The mechanical bridge has been around for a long time. Numerous varieties and types are available. The last few years have brought an explosion of new bridges, as it seems that everyone has tried to come up with the perfect mechanical bridge. This situation may have come about when players realized that some shots were too far away to reach.

There was a time when it was legal to get up onto the table and shoot your shot. There is a famous picture of Larry Johnson (Boston Shorty) lying across a pool table at the Johnson City tournament during the 1960s. The rules nowadays do not allow that. You must have one foot on the floor when executing a shot. This rule may have been created after a few

### *Mechanical Bridge*

- The mechanical bridge is used when you are unable to reach a shot.

- You want to have your shooting arm parallel to the table. This position will allow a straight follow-through.

- Place your other hand on top of the handle so that the bridge doesn't move.

- Use an open stance. Concentrate on making the shot and do not try to do too much as far as moving the cue ball around the table.

### *Double Bridges*

- Double bridges are used in rare cases.

- They are used when the cue ball is out of reach and a group of balls lies in front of the cue ball.

- Place one bridge on top of another and make sure they are firmly together. Firmly

- hold down the butt end of the bridge on the playing surface with your non-shooting hand.

- The sticks must be on the playing surface for good stability.

of the larger players got up onto the table, and either the slate broke or the table went out of level.

Some players shoot behind their back to avoid using the mechanical bridge. Confident professional players often showcase this technique.

Using a mechanical bridge is the part of the game that players practice the least. Knowing the correct way to shoot and aim with a mechanical bridge is a must. Mastering this shot is important. At some point it will be the difference between winning and losing.

The best mechanical bridge players are the ones who grew up playing Snooker. Snooker is played on a 12-by-6-foot table. Because of its enormous size, the mechanical bridge is used often.

The bridge has a few nicknames, such as the "granny stick" and "the crutch."

## Stance Using the Bridge

- As mentioned, your feet should be a comfortable distance apart, 18 to 24 inches.

- Your stance will be more upright when using a bridge because the bridge head is higher than a normal hand bridge would be.

- Use an open stance, which means that the front of your body needs to face the table.

- Maintain your balance all the way through the shot.

## Stroking with a Bridge

- Many players tend to use a punch stroke when shooting with a bridge.

- Do not drop your elbow during the shot. For accuracy and consistency, it must remain parallel to the table.

- The back of your cue will be more elevated during these shots, which will make it a bit more difficult to aim.

- You want to use a smooth stroke and center ball hits.

# STROKE

## Another element needed to help improve your game is a good stroke

The perfect stroke is something every player strives for. The stroke is a combination of the hand, body, and cue stick working as one to make solid contact with the cue ball. The more fluid the stroke, the better it is. This means that you are relaxed and confident.

You can use many kinds of strokes. The players with the smooth stroke are usually the better shooters. Every sport has players who have great strokes and bad strokes. The better your stroke is, the better you will perform under pressure.

If you practice with good techniques, you will notice that the more often you play, the more your stroke improves. The more your stroke improves, the better you will play. When

### Pendulum Effect

- You need to create a pendulum effect; the only movement should be in your shooting arm.

- If you get your shoulders or body involved in the shot, you will lose that level stroke and increase your chances of a miss.

- Watch very good players. You can learn from the way they approach their shots.

- For best results video yourself and watch for the pendulum effect.

### Practice Strokes and Smooth Backstroke

- You should take three to five practice strokes on every shot.

- After more than five practice strokes (except in some special situations), you lose concentration.

- With fewer than three, you are not yet prepared to shoot the shot.

- Every shot, including the easiest ones, needs to be executed properly.

you can get everything working as one, you will feel your confidence grow. Players who do not practice good techniques will progress more slowly.

Some of the greatest players in the world come from the Philippines. The secret to their success is their unique stroke. Their stroke has much more motion than the stroke of most other professionals. They have adapted that stroke to their game with tremendous success.

Practice your stroke by stroking your cue through the opening of a soda bottle. If your stroke is not fluid and straight, you will hit the sides of the bottle. It is a great way to practice your motions.

You can also learn about strokes by watching professional golfers putting the ball. They want to have a good rhythm to their stroke when they putt. They also follow through and keep their head still. These same techniques apply to shooting pool.

## Stay Down Follow-through

- Keep your head still during the shot. Do not lift your head during or right after you strike the cue ball.

- You need to have a good follow-through. This goes along with having a fluid stroke.

- The cue stick should extend out a few inches past where the cue ball was. Listen for the ball to drop into the pocket.

- If you find yourself jumping up after each shot, practice staying down until the ball falls into the pocket.

## Fluid Motion

- A good stroke should feel like you have a crumpled-up piece of paper in your hand and want to throw it underhanded into a basket.

- The stroke requires a fluid motion, just like what you want to have when shooting a shot. Use this as a mental tool when you practice.

- Your stroke will continue to improve over time. Keep practicing.

# BASIC AIMING TECHNIQUES

If you want to beat your buddies in the game of pool, read this section carefully

The main purposes of basic cue ball control are to keep from scratching, to control the cue ball, and to play position. To advance your game to the next level, you need to learn the basics of aiming and cue ball control. For many years players simply went up to the table and shot balls without knowing what happened during the shot. This was true for both amateurs and top-level players because they were self-taught and pocketing balls just came naturally to them. After years of practice, instinct taught them where to hit the ball so it would go into the pocket.

Today's top players are much more knowledgeable and understand what the cue ball will do in almost every situation.

## Ghost Ball

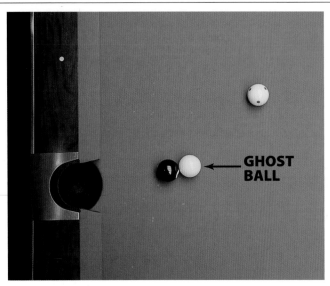

GHOST BALL ←

- The ghost ball is an imaginary cue ball that shows the location the cue ball will need to be in order to pocket the object ball

- There are different training tools available, like aimers, to help you visualize the shot with the ghost ball.

- Many players have used the ghost ball as a training method for years.

- As shown in the picture, the plain cue ball represents the ghost ball. The spotted cue ball is your starting point.

## Contact Points

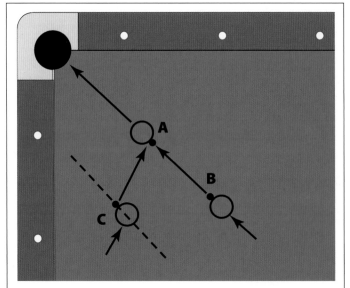

- Contact points are where the cue ball and object ball touch.

- The contact point is the part on the object ball (A) that is the farthest from the pocket.

- The only time the contact point is through the center of the cue and object ball is on a straight-in shot. (B)

- (C) is the contact point on the cue ball when shooting from an angle.

Having an understanding of how the cue ball will react to different hits allows you to advance at a much faster rate.

Here is a good test: The next time you are at your buddy's house, ask if he knows how to hit a stop shot and what the cue ball has to do in order for it to happen. Most players do not know the answer to this question. But by understanding what really happens, you can execute the shot much more easily and with far greater control. The more you know, the faster you will learn.

Today many training tools and methods help with aiming.

All players progress at a different rate. For some players aiming comes naturally, and they advance quickly. Others need to work much harder on this part of the game. This is true in every sport.

## Eye Movement

- Your eyes need to be in line with the cue stick, cue ball, and object ball.

- Your eyes should focus back and forth between the cue and object ball on your practice strokes.

- During your entire shot you need to keep the head as still as possible.

- Your last look should be at the object ball, not the cue ball.

## Dominant Eye

- One way to determine your dominant eye is to cut a hole in a piece of paper and hold it at arm's length.

- Focus on an object and then close each eye one at a time.

- When you see the object appear centered in the circle, you are using the dominant eye.

- Because the non-dominant eye will see objects at a slight angle, it is best to keep your dominant eye in line with your cue stick.

# BASIC CUE BALL CONTROL

## If you learn the basics, you will be on your way to becoming a better player

If you want to take your game to the next level, it is strongly recommended that you take lessons from a knowledgeable instructor. Many pool instructors stress that the most important aspect of the game is control of the cue ball. After you have mastered this part of the game, there is nothing to stop you from becoming a really good player. Without cue ball

control, you will never be able to pocket more than one or two balls except on rare occasions.

Have you ever watched the pros on television? Someone once commented, "The pros aren't that good. Every shot they make is an easy one." Of course, their shots are easy. The reason is simple: They put the cue ball in the perfect position

### Stop Shot

- A stop shot is when the cue ball does not move after contacting the object ball. It requires a center or below-center hit on the cue ball, depending on the distance.

- The cue ball needs to be sliding when it makes contact with the object ball.

- It cannot have follow or draw upon contact.

- Use more speed or a lower hit on the cue ball to get a stop shot as the distance between the cue and the object ball increases.

### Draw

- To apply draw on the cue ball, a below-center hit is necessary.

- As a beginner, you should go no more than one tip below center of the cue ball (as seen in the photo above) until you become comfortable and proficient with that stroke.

- Draw on a straight-in shot makes the cue ball effectively come back toward you, depending on how hard and how low you hit the cue ball.

every time to make the next shot. This represents excellent cue ball control.

You may never get to the level of a pro, but you can get good enough to string together some nice runs. You will be amazed by how good you can get when you know how to control the cue ball.

## Follow

- Applying follow to the cue ball requires an above-center hit. The cue ball will roll forward after contact with the object ball.

- For beginners, a follow shot is much easier to learn and control than a draw shot.

- The amount of follow on the cue ball is determined by tip placement, power, and distance between balls.

- Keep your stick as level as possible when applying follow.

## Left and Right English

- The main purpose of English is to change the angle of the cue ball off the cushions (also known as rails) for position play.

- When applying English, visualize the cue ball as a clock. Left is at nine o'clock, and right is at three o'clock

from the center of the cue ball.

- The same applies to English as follow and draw. When positioning on the cue, you should go no more than one tip away from the center of the cue ball.

29

# CONTROLLING SPEED

## Knowing the speed of the table is necessary for good position play

You will play on many makes and models of pool tables. Some of the tables will play faster than others. This means that the cue ball and object balls will roll for a longer distance on some and a shorter distance on others with the same hit applied.

The type of cloth used, how well the cloth was put on and stretched out, and the bounce off the rails will determine the speed of the table. Hit your normal speed for a lag shot a few times to help you determine if a table is faster or slower than you're used to. You will then need to make adjustments during your game. The lag will also let you know if the table is level. By knowing these little things, you increase your chances of beating your buddies or winning a tournament.

You should create a warm up routine every time you play on a different table. Doing so will make it easier for you to make adjustments.

### Thin Cuts

- The thinner you cut a ball, the farther the cue ball will travel after the hit.

- Keep in mind that a thin hit will require less speed on the cue ball to achieve the desired position.

- This type of shot requires a lot of practice to get the correct feel for it.

- It is sometimes better to play defense on a shot that requires a very thin cut because thin cut shots are difficult shots to make.

### Full Hit

- A full hit is when the cue ball hits the object ball straight on. The fuller the hit on an object ball, the less distance the cue ball will travel.

- You will need to increase your power accordingly to get the cue ball in position for the next shot.

- Keep in mind that shooting the cue ball hard decreases your chances of pocketing the ball.

- The stop shot is easier to execute when using a full hit.

Anytime you have extra knowledge about the playing conditions, you have gained an edge on your opponent. This slight edge could be the difference between winning and losing.

Practice cut shots with the object ball in different positions on the table. Put the object ball near a corner pocket and practice speed control as the cue ball bounces off the rail. Practice your speed control from other positions, such as hitting the cue ball 3 rails around the table or banking the cue ball cross side. This will also help you get a feel for the rails.

## Short and Long Bridges

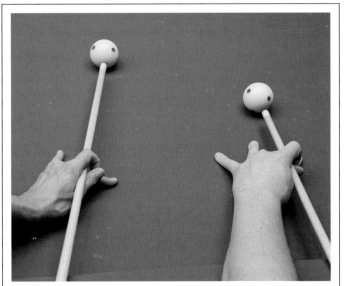

- A long bridge is used mostly for power shots and breaking.

- With a long bridge you will give up control on the cue ball.

- A short bridge may stick out only 3 to 4 inches beyond your bridge hand. This is used only on close shots where it is not required to move the cue ball very far.

- Short bridges are better for delicate and softer hits on the cue ball.

### Controlling Speed

To practice your speed control, lag the cue ball to the far end of the table and have it come back toward you. Keep the following in mind:

- Practice using follow and draw.

- Concentrate.

- Maintain good practice sessions.

- Practice shooting at different distances.

# OBJECT BALL HITS

## Mentally break down the object ball into fractions to create good habits for aiming

Someone once said that trying to hit one round object into another round object is one of the most difficult things you can do. This person was referring to baseball, but it also applies to pool. Because the cue ball and the object ball are round, it is difficult to describe to a student or new player where he or she needs to aim. The easiest way to teach

players where the cue ball needs to contact the object ball is by using fractions such as ¼ or ½. This mental image helps beginner players understand the concept of aiming on the object ball.

When you factor in all the other variables in the game of pool, such as English and table conditions, knowing where to

### Full Ball Hit

- A full ball hit is when the cue ball is shot straight into the object ball.

- On a full ball hit, in most cases you will use only top, bottom, or center on the cue ball.

- If you have trouble getting a full ball hit, you will need to check your alignment.

- A full ball hit is one of the easiest to recognize.

### Three-quarter Ball Hit

- In a three-quarter ball hit you aim to have three-quarters of the cue ball cover the surface of the object ball.

- Simply divide the object ball into four equal parts.

- Have the cue ball cover three of the four parts when it makes contact with the object ball.

- The cue ball will travel a shorter distance than the object ball.

aim on the ball to make your shot can get very confusing. In addition to beginner players and even experienced players, many trick shot artists use this fractions method more than any other when performing trick shots to ensure accuracy and the completion of their tricks.

## Half Ball Hit

- After the full ball hit, the next easiest to recognize is the half ball hit.

- It is easy to line up because half of the cue ball hits half of the object ball.

- This shot seems to come up more often than any of the other hits.

- In most cases the cue ball and the object ball will travel about the same distance after contact.

## One-quarter Ball Hit

- One-quarter ball hits are used when you are trying to move the object ball a short distance and the cue ball a longer one.

- These hits are used for thin hits on the object ball and can be used both offensively and defensively.

- The one-quarter ball hit is the reversal of the three-quarter ball hit.

- You want the cue ball to cover one-quarter of the object ball on contact.

# LEFT & RIGHT ENGLISH
## At times a center ball hit just won't get you to where you need to go

Applying left- and right-hand English to the cue ball is one of the most interesting parts of the game—and probably one of the most confusing. This section covers the basics of English; more in-depth chapters follow later in the book.

Anytime you have the chance to use a center ball hit, you should do so. Center ball hits decrease your chance of miscuing. A miscue happens when your tip slips off the cue ball during your shot. It will make a sound that you will soon take a disliking to. Most miscues occur when players apply too much English to the cue ball.

To apply English, you need to hit to either the left or right of the center of the cue ball. The farther your tip is from the center, the more English you will apply and the more your cue ball will spin. It will also increase your chances of a miscue.

*Left/Right, Angle 1*

- Start out with a distance of about 2 feet between the cue ball and the object ball.

- Apply one-quarter tip of right English.

- Aim for the ball to go directly into the center of the pocket.

- Shoot the ball into the pocket with enough speed to just make it to the opposite end of the table.

- Shoot the shot from the opposite side of the table and do the same using left English.

*Left/Right, Angle 2*

- Keep the same 2-foot distance between the cue ball and the object ball along with the same angle.

- Apply one-quarter tip of right English to the cue ball.

- Aim for the ball to go directly into the center of the pocket.

- Shoot the ball into the pocket with enough speed to come all the way back to the short rail near where you started from.

With the tips and chalk available today, you will be able to execute these types of shots more consistently. This is one of the many reasons to chalk up before each shot.

If you are just starting out and want to experiment with using English on the cue ball, aim your cue about a half tip to the right of the center of the cue ball. You will need to practice making balls with the tip in this position. Again, working with two round objects gets a bit confusing, but with practice it will become more and more natural to you. Some

other variables are involved. They will be covered in a later chapter.

## *Left/Right, Angle 3*

- Start out with a distance of about 2 feet between the cue ball and the object ball.

- Apply a half tip of right English.

- Aim for the ball to go directly into the center of the pocket.

- Hit with enough speed for the cue ball to travel to the far end of the table. Do the same using left English.

## *Left/Right, Angle 4*

- Keep the same 2-foot distance between the cue ball and the object ball along with the same angle.

- Apply a half tip of right English to the cue ball.

- Aim for the ball to go directly into the center of the pocket.

- Hit with enough speed for the cue ball to go around the table and return to the short rail closest to where you started the shot from.

# MORE CUE BALL CONTROL
## Going farther from the center of the cue ball is necessary for some shots

Basic cue ball hits were discussed in the previous sections. You need to practice these hits before going on to the more difficult ones. After you feel comfortable with your technique, and you can make a high percentage of your shots, you can move on to the next step.

Applying both follow and draw with left or right English on

a shot can get a bit tricky. It will require much practice.

Again, this is another variable that goes into making the shot. Each time you add something to a shot, your "make percentage" will go down.

When you think about a pool table, depending on its size, you are talking about a small area. It is not like in golf, soccer,

### Left/Right/Top/Bottom, Angle 1

- Keep the distance of the cue ball to the object ball at about 2 feet.

- Aim for the shot to go into the center of the corner pocket.

- Aim your cue one-quarter tip to the right of center and a half tip down from the center of the cue ball.

- Hit the shot hard enough for the cue ball to travel to the short rail at the far end of the table.

### Left/Right/Top/Bottom, Angle 2

- Keep the distance of the cue ball to the object ball at about 2 feet.

- Aim for the shot to go into the center of the corner pocket.

- Aim your cue a half tip to the right of the center and a half tip down from the center of the cue ball.

- Hit the shot hard enough for the cue ball to travel to the short rail at the far end of the table.

football, or baseball, where you have plenty of room. Every shot in pool really does come down to a game of inches or, actually, fractions of an inch. For this reason you must be able to put the cue ball into what is sometimes a very small opening. To accomplish this, you need to learn how to apply more than one type of English on a shot.

## Left/Right/Top/Bottom, Angle 3

- Keep the distance of the cue ball to the object ball at about 2 feet.

- Aim for the shot to go into the center of the corner pocket.

- Aim your cue one-quarter tip to the right of the center and a half tip down from the center of the cue ball.

- Hit the shot hard enough for the cue ball to travel all the way back to the short rail nearest to where the shot started from.

## Left/Right/Top/Bottom, Angle 4

- Keep the distance of the cue ball to the object ball at about 2 feet.

- Aim for the shot to go into the center of the corner pocket.

- Aim your cue a half tip to the right of the center and a half tip down from the center of the cue ball.

- Hit the shot hard enough for the cue ball to travel all the way back to the short rail nearest to where the shot started from.

# ADVANCED CUE BALL CONTROL

## You have all the basics mastered, but there is still much more to learn

Again we go back to the subject of hitting one round object with another round object. When you shoot, you are hitting the first round object with a leather tip attached to a piece of wood that's also known as a "cue stick." Throw in chalk and humidity, and you have created a whole new set of variables that affects how you shoot.

With all of the variables that go into shooting, it's no wonder that many players have no idea why they miss a shot. Sometimes they miss a shot because of simple, basic factors, such as alignment or aiming. At other times they miss a shot because they lacked control of an advanced shot.

Many players ask, "How do you aim when you put English

### Deflection

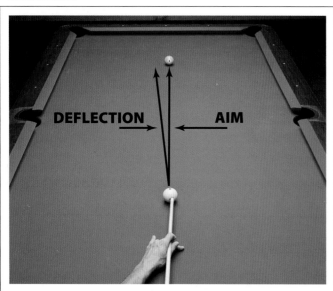

- Deflection is the reaction of the cue ball and the path it takes when right or left English is applied to a shot.

- The cue ball deflects to the right when left English is applied.

- The cue ball deflects to the left when right English is applied.

- The more speed and English applied to the cue ball, the more deflection will occur.

### Test for Deflection

- To test for deflection, put the cue ball on the head spot.

- Have your tip at three o'clock on the cue ball. Aim for the center diamond at the far end of the table.

- Shoot the ball firmly at the center diamond.

- Check to see how far to the left or right of the center diamond the cue ball hits the rail.

on the cue ball?" Applying English to the cue ball makes it react in different ways as you will see described below. After you have learned to pocket balls, applying English will be the number one cause of most of your misses. Even the most seasoned players sometimes miss shots when applying English.

## Controlling Deflection

- The shaft on your cue stick will affect how much deflection will occur.

- If you change to a new shaft that has less deflection in it, you will need to practice with it first.

- Your aiming point will be different with the new shaft. You will need to make adjustments.

- Shafts built for less deflection cost more than regular replacement shafts.

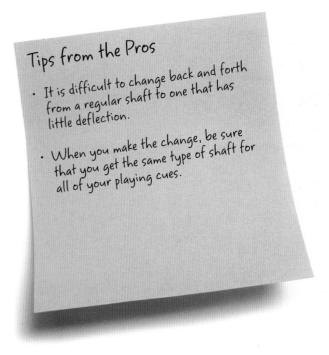

*Tips from the Pros*

- It is difficult to change back and forth from a regular shaft to one that has little deflection.

- When you make the change, be sure that you get the same type of shaft for all of your playing cues.

ADVANCED SKILLS

39

# CURVE & MASSÉ

## If your shot is blocked, and you can't bank or jump at it, try the massé

The next time you walk into your local pool room, look around for a sign about massé shots. If a pool room owner does not allow them, somewhere in that room will be a sign stating so.

To massé you need to put extreme English on the cue ball. There are both vertical and level massé strokes. Most players resort to the massé shot as a last-ditch effort to make a good

hit on a ball. It is the hardest stroke in all of pool to control.

This is not a shot for beginners. When attempted by an inexperienced player, the massé stroke could easily rip the cloth on a table.

You can purchase a specialty cue made just for the full vertical massé shot. The massé cue, like the jump cue, is shorter,

### Slightly Elevated Massé

- There are times when you need to curve the cue ball a slight amount to go around one ball and hit your object ball.

- Slightly elevate the back of your cue. Do not grip the cue too tightly.

- Aim far enough outside your normal target line so that the cue ball can pass by the blocker ball.

- Hit the cue ball with a firm punch stroke. Practice is the only way to learn how much the cue ball will curve.

### Massé Follow

- With the cue ball frozen to the rail and the 8 ball, you can hit a massé follow shot and make the cue ball curve around the 8 ball.

- Elevate the butt end of the cue stick about 6 inches. Aim about 4 inches to the right of the 5 ball.

- Hit at eleven o'clock on the cue ball with a firm stroke to create extreme top spin and make the cue ball curve as it goes down the table.

- It will pass the 8 ball and make the 5 ball in the corner and the 8 ball will follow into the same corner.

but it is much heavier. It can weigh up to 25 ounces. The extra weight helps provide the power necessary to create the extreme spin that the tip puts on the cue ball.

Properly executing the massé shot takes many months of practice. If you find yourself wanting to learn this shot, you should start on a table on which you plan to change the cloth in the near future.

A slightly elevated massé shot, in which you only elevate the butt end of the cue a small amount, is a much more controlled shot versus the vertical massé.

## Curve Using Draw

- To curve the cue ball around another ball, you hit into the rail with draw.

- Aim the tip at six o'clock on the cue ball. Have a loose back hand grip.

- Hit the cue ball with a firm stroke. It is important to hit very low on the cue ball.

- The cue ball will come off the rail and curve. The amount of curve will depend on how much draw and speed are applied.

## Full Vertical Massé

- Caution! Start off with soft hits until you have perfected the technique.

- It is best to use a massé cue for better control.

- Hold the massé cue straight up in the air with the tip aimed at the outside edge of the cue ball.

- Hit straight down and into the cloth. Damage to the cloth occurs when the tip comes in at an angle. Properly executed massé shots will not damage a cloth unless numerous repetitions are shot from the same spot.

ADVANCED SKILLS

# THROW

## Knowing how to make an object ball "throw" will help you win more often

Pool players of all experience levels can widely overlook the throw shot. Because this shot will come into play many times during your game, it is important to have an understanding of this shot. When you show your friends how to apply throw to a ball, they will be impressed.

At exhibitions many top players demonstrate different types of shots that come up in a typical pool game. The throw shot is one of the easiest to teach.

To "throw" a ball simply means to change the direction of an object ball by using friction or by applying English. When two balls are frozen together or even when there is a small gap between them, you can change the normal path that

*Throw with Two Balls Frozen*

- When you have two balls frozen together, you can alter the normal path of the object ball.

- The cue ball needs to contact the first ball and push it in the direction of the side pocket.

- Hitting the right side of the 1 ball will throw the 2 ball to the left and make it in the side pocket.

- The amount of throw will vary on different tables.

*Throw Two Balls with a Slight Gap*

- When two balls are close together and there is a slight gap between them, you can still throw the ball into the corner pocket.

- The same method applies here as with two balls that are frozen.

- Shoot the cue ball into the back ball. Try to get a full hit on the ball.

- The object ball will move slightly forward and go into the pocket.

the balls would take. For example, when cutting a ball to the right, even if there is a substantial distance between the cue ball and the object ball, left English on the cue ball will give you slightly more cut on the object ball. The more spin on the cue ball, the more cut on the object ball.

One caveat: It is harder to put throw on a set of balls that has just been polished. You will actually get more throw with a set of balls that has not been polished in a while. The reason is that a polished ball will not create as much friction. Moisture also affects how much a ball throws. If the room is very humid, the object ball will have less throw. Speed also affects the amount of throw on a ball. The harder you shoot, the less it throws.

## Cue Ball Throw

- When the cue ball and the object ball are frozen together, you can alter the path of the object ball.

- One of the ways to do this is to aim in the direction you want the object ball to throw.

- Simply shoot the cue ball away from the frozen ball.

- The object ball will move slightly forward with the cue ball and go into the pocket.

## Cue Ball Throw Using English

- When the cue ball and the object ball are frozen together, you can alter the path of the object ball with English.

- If you want the object ball to go to the right, apply left English. If you want the object ball to go to the left, apply right English.

- Elevate the butt end of your cue stick and hit this shot with right English using a punch stroke.

- The object ball will curve toward the direction of the pocket.

# JUMP SHOTS

## If you can't go around a ball, you may need to hit a jump shot

When you first start playing with jump shots, you need to be taught the proper technique by a more experienced player. Novice players may try scooping under the cue ball to make it jump over another ball; however, this method is neither legal nor good for the cloth. When you scoop the cue ball, you have no control over it.

The jump shot may easily become a player's favorite shot to play. The availability of jump cues allows just about anyone to learn how to hit a legal jump shot. Jump cues are light and have a hard tip on them. This construction creates a bounce effect and allows the tip to quickly get out of the way after the cue ball is struck. Hitting down on the cue ball into the slate makes the cue ball jump. A wide variety of jump cues are available. In trick shot exhibitions, players carry several jump cues. Some of the cues are for short, high jumps; others are designed to jump the cue ball a long distance.

### Tip Placement for Jump Shot

- For a normal jump shot, you want to aim your tip slightly below center of the cue ball.

- Holding the back end of the cue lightly, hit the cue ball with a firm punch stroke.

- You should feel like you are throwing the cue stick at the ball.

- This will create the bounce effect, which then pulls the tip back and out of the way.

### Cue Angle for Jump Shot

- The longer the jump, the more level the stick needs to be. This angle will send the cue ball on a lower trajectory.

- When you are close to the blocking ball that you need to jump over, you need to increase the elevation of the back end of your cue.

- It is a common mistake to overelevate the cue during a jump shot.

- Be aware of the angle of the cue by looking at where it crosses your body.

Jump cues are not allowed at many tournaments and in some leagues. Before using your jump cue, ask if it is allowed.

········· YELLOW ● LIGHT ·········

For maximum jump, you need to have a loose grip with your back hand. The lighter the cue and the harder the tip, the easier it is to hit a jump shot. Some players jump with a conventional grip, whereas others use the dart-style grip. It is harder to jump with a full playing cue because of its weight, balance, and softer tip.

## Grip for Jump Shot

- The looser the grip, the more action there will be on the jump. Gripping too tightly on the cue will take away from the bounce effect you are trying to create.

- Both a regular grip and a forehand grip are used for jumping. The choice is a personal preference.

- The forehand grip (player on left in photo) is used more often for short and close jumps.

- The regular grip (player on right) is better for longer, more powerful jumps.

## Jump Shot in Action

- The path of the jump shot depends on power, angle of the cue, and the thickness of the slate.

- Having control of the jump shot will come with practice.

- When starting out, be careful of people and objects around the pool table.

- When jumping with a full cue, you need to hit the cue ball harder. You also will not get as much jump.

# TANGENT LINES

## One of the most misunderstood aspects of the game is the physics of tangent lines

With the exception of top players, few understand what the tangent line is. Basically, it is the path that the ball takes after it makes contact with another ball. This understanding is necessary if you want to advance your game.

Whenever there is a cluster of balls on the table, knowledge of the tangent line is invaluable. It will give you opportunities to pocket balls that you may not have realized before. Knowing the tangent line will also make you a better defensive player.

One of the easiest ways to find the tangent line is to place a pencil behind two frozen balls. Have the pencil touch both balls. Take another pencil and form a 90-degree angle

## Tangent Line

- The tangent line runs at a 90-degree angle through the center of the two balls where they touch.

- Knowing the tangent line is important when shooting all shots.

- The path follows the edge of the ball, not the center of the ball.

- Learn to recognize and understand the tangent line to increase your skill level both offensively and defensively.

*Understanding Tangent Lines*

**TANGENT LINE**

- Shoot the cue ball into the 8 ball. The right edge of the 8 ball will follow the tangent line.

- Shoot this shot with a soft to medium speed and a center or high ball hit.

- If you shoot too hard or apply draw, the 8 ball will go to the right of the original tangent line shown.

- This will depend on how hard or how much draw is applied to the shot.

touching the first pencil between the two balls. This will show you the tangent line. The edge of the ball will travel along the tangent line. After you have done this test a few times, you can quickly see the tangent line without the help of the pencils.

Here's a good practice session: Freeze two balls together and line up the tangent line so that the ball will pocket in the corner. Hit the shot and watch where the object ball goes. By doing this, you will get a better understanding of direction. You can also apply follow and draw and watch how they affect the path of the object ball. You will soon become good at locating the exact tangent line for every shot. Knowing tangent lines allows you to control the cue ball and become a better position player. You will be amazed at how quickly your game will improve.

## Carom Tangent Lines

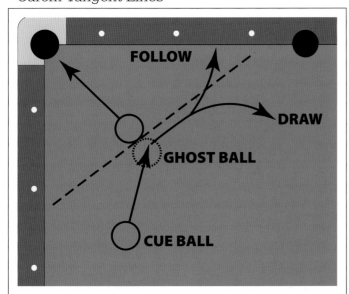

- When you shoot a carom shot, the cue ball will start off on the tangent line when it leaves the object ball.

- The distance the cue ball stays on the tangent line depends on the speed you hit the shot with and if you apply draw or follow.

- For example, you will notice how long the cue ball stays on the tangent line with a soft, medium, and hard shot.

- Also, the direction will depend on whether you use draw, follow, or center ball hit.

## Object Ball Tangent Lines

- The more balls that are involved in the shot, the more the tangent line will change.

- The reason is that you will have more resistance due to the weight of the extra balls.

- The more weight or resistance involved in the tangent line, the more the path of the original tangent line will change.

- When shooting a shot involving multiple balls, you will need to adjust accordingly.

# CAROMS & COMBINATIONS

## Combination shots are more difficult than they appear, and carom shots are not shot often enough

Caroms and combinations will come up many times during the course of a game. Unless the combination shot is straight in or an object ball is close to a pocket, you should avoid shooting it. The greater the distance between two balls, the more difficult the combination shot is.

Combination shots require your full attention. Even the simplest combination shot should not be taken for granted. You can use different approaches when lining up these shots. The key to executing a combination shot is to stay committed to it. Too many times players get down on a shot and change their aiming point at the last second. If you find yourself in this situation, stand up and start over.

*Two-ball Combination*

- Combination shots are always more difficult than they appear. Try to avoid any combination shots where a large gap exists between the balls.

- Carefully line up the combination shot. You need to visualize the second ball as if it were the cue ball. That is the path it needs to take.

- Stay down and commit to the shot.

- Avoid using English on the cue ball unless it is absolutely necessary.

*Long Combination Shot*

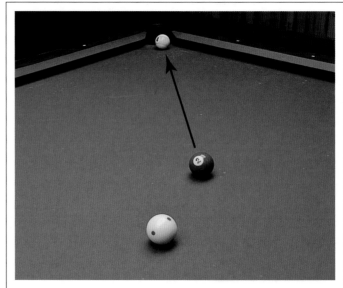

- There will be opportunities, especially in 9-ball, where you can end the game early with a combination shot.

- When the object ball is hanging near the pocket, and you can get a good angle to play the combination, you should go for it.

- The closer the object ball is to the pocket, the easier the combination shot is.

- Shoot the cue ball into the 2 ball and play the 2 ball as if you were trying to pocket it in the corner.

Carom shots are more difficult to recognize for the average player. A carom shot is when you deflect one ball off another ball. After you learn how to tell if a carom shot will go into the pocket, you can find shots you never knew existed before. To make carom shots consistently, you will need to know about tangent lines (see page 46).

(see page 46)

## *Carom Shot*

- When two balls are frozen or close together, a carom shot is a great way to pocket a ball.

- You need to check the tangent line to make sure the ball will go.

- Hit the cue ball into the first ball to create the correct tangent line for pocketing the ball.

- You can also carom the cue ball into another ball to pocket an object ball.

## *Cue Ball Carom*

- In a game of 9-Ball, this carom shot will win you the game. Simply carom the cue ball off the 1 ball to pocket the 9.

- Carom shots are a great tool for both offense and defense.

- Carom shots are not practiced nearly enough. The more you understand and practice carom shots, the easier it is to find the correct aiming point on your first object ball.

ADVANCED SKILLS

# BANKING SYSTEMS

## There are many ways to figure out where to aim when shooting a bank or kick shot

If you want to get to the winner's circle, you have to know your banks and kicks. Knowing these will get you out of trouble and help you to avoid fouling. One of the worst mistakes you can make is to give ball-in-hand to your opponent, especially in 8-Ball and 9-Ball. Ball-in-hand occurs when your opponent can take the cue ball and place it anywhere on the

table, and it typically occurs after a scratch.

Have you ever seen a player lining up a bank shot walk to the other side of the table to try to figure out the correct angle? Unless he looks to see if there is enough clearance for the object ball to pass by, he will have a difficult time figuring out the angle. Here's why: First, by the time he steps back

### Diamond System

- The diamonds are the markers located on the rails around the table.

- The diamonds are used to help calculate bank and kick shots. By knowing the diamond system, you can more easily determine the natural angle of a shot.

- There are numerous methods for using the diamond system, none of which are easy to learn.

- The diamond system is used mostly in Three-cushion billiards because every shot is a bank or kick shot involving three or more rails.

### Mirror Systems

- Imagine another pool table right alongside the one you are playing on.

- You then want to aim the banking ball into the corner pocket of the imaginary table.

- Put a mirror on the rail as shown in the picture.

- The mirror on the rail will allow you to see the pocket. Just aim the object ball into the pocket. This will help you learn the mirror system.

around to the other side to shoot, he probably has forgotten where to aim. Second, most calculations for banking and kicking are done when addressing the cue ball.

Have you wondered what those diamonds on the rail are used for? There are six diamonds on the long rails and three diamonds on the short rails that help calculate banks and kicks. But take note: The problem with the diamond system is that no two tables play alike. Also, most of the systems are very complicated and will take some time to master. To use the diamond system correctly, you would first have to test out the table to see if it is playing long, short, or right on. You would then need to make the proper adjustments in your shots.

## *Equal Angle*

- When you shoot a shot, the object ball will come off the rail in the same angle as it went into the rail.

- You can use this method for both one-rail and two-rail bank shots.

- A good way to judge the angle and path of the object ball is to use your cue as a guide. Line up from the cue to the object ball to the rail.

- Then move your stick to the opposite and equal angle on the other side to see where the object ball goes.

# FACTORS AFFECTING ANGLES

## A wide variety of factors determine angles

No two pool tables play exactly alike. The reason is that the rubber on the rails and the cloth on the table are not exactly the same. One table may be used more than another. There may be more humidity around one table than another. All of these factors affect the angle at which a ball leaves a rail.

Many homeowners place pool tables in the basement of their house. Other homes do not have basements, and the pool table is found on the main level of the house. Basements,

depending on the age of the house and the type of insulation and heating used, will make a difference in how a table plays. Even if the table is located on the main level, many factors, including heating, air conditioning, and the degree to which windows are open, will affect the rails. Precipitation is a major factor in how a rail shot will play.

Rails are made of rubber that reacts to different temperatures and conditions. Think of the wintertime on a cold day.

Factors Affecting Angles

- Speed of stroke
- English
- Cut angle
- Humidity
- Condition of tables
- Condition of rubber on the rails

### Speed of Stroke

TOO SOFT

TOO HARD

- Speed affects a bank shot more than anything else.

- Speed must be accurate to make an object ball bank naturally.

- The harder you shoot, the more the bank shot will shorten up, making the

object ball bank at a narrow angle and causing you to miss the shot.

- Shooting too hard will make the 1 ball come up short of the side pocket. Shooting too soft will bank the 1 ball long.

Cold contracts rubber and makes it much harder. When the temperature is warm, rubber expands and becomes softer. Having your table in a temperature-controlled area will make the rails play much truer. If you do have your table in an area of high humidity, try using a dehumidifier. It will help to absorb the moisture from the air.

For most tables the difference in the reaction off the rail will be only a small amount unless the table is in an area of extreme temperature changes. To help diffuse these variables, manufacturers now offer indoor-outdoor tables. These tables are well designed and are found frequently on lanais in the South.

## Using English

- When applying English on the cue ball, the direction of the object ball will change slightly off the cushion.

- English will not shorten the angle as much as speed will unless the object ball is close to the cushion.

- When you shoot into the object ball with English, the effect will be a slight amount of opposite English on the object ball.

- The farther the object ball travels, the less chance of it having English.

## Cut Angle

- Cutting an object ball causes side spin.

- The cut actually transfers English on the object ball.

- When you cut the object ball to the right, it transfers left English on the object ball. To compensate, you would need to cut the 1 ball thin here.

- Shoot with a medium hard stroke so the English doesn't die out before the object ball contacts the cushion.

# CHANGING ANGLES ON KICKS

## Sometimes you need to kick at a ball, and you need to change the natural angle

A kick shot is used when you can't see the object ball and have to shoot the cue ball into the rail and kick at it in an attempt to get a good hit. Every player tries to avoid giving up ball-in-hand. By learning how to control your kick shots, you increase your chances of winning.

When you play someone who likes to use lots of defense, the need for kick shots will come up often, and you need to be prepared. Knowing how to change the angle at which the cue ball rebounds off the rail when executing a kick shot will get you out of many difficult situations.

The first players to use the kicking system with control were the Filipinos. Efren Reyes, considered by many as the greatest

*Kicking Using Follow*

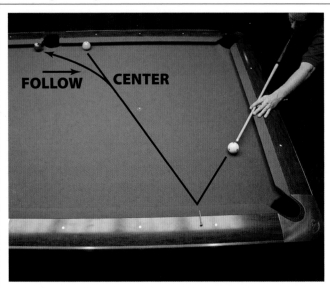

*Kicking Using Draw*

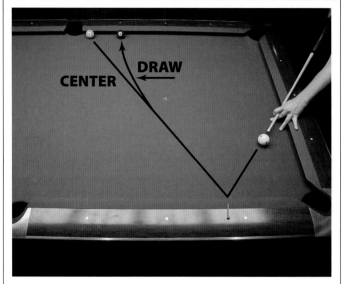

- When shooting into the cushion with follow, the cue ball will rebound at a longer angle than if you used a center ball hit.

- The 2 ball in the photo is where the cue ball will hit when using follow.

- The 1 ball is where the cue ball will hit when using a center ball hit.

- The width of the angle depends on how high you shoot on the cue ball and how much speed you use.

- When you shoot the cue ball below center with a draw stroke, the effect will be the opposite of follow.

- The cue ball will rebound at a narrower angle than when you use an above center hit.

- The resulting angle will depend on how low you shoot on the cue ball and how hard you stroke.

- When you shoot with a softer stroke, the cue ball will curve sooner than when you use a medium or hard stroke.

pool player ever, was one of the first players to kick at balls and play safe at the same time. It is no wonder he has the nickname "the Magician." Soon after Efren started to kick at balls with control, everyone else worked on that part of the game.

By applying different English on the cue ball, you can change its path. Only practice will help you learn how to control the cue ball during a kick shot.

You need to learn the table before you can control the kick shot. Some tables play longer or shorter than others. If you can, test the table before you play. Hit the cue ball three rails where you normally would to pocket it in the corner near you. If it goes to the long rail side of the corner pocket, that means the table is playing short and you need to adjust.

## English and Speed

- This is a good example of how English affects the rebound off the cushion.

- Although speed affects the angle similar to banking, English has much more effect on the cue ball than does speed.

- When shooting into the cushion with English, the softer the stoke you use, the more the cue ball will grab and widen the angle.

- When shooting hard here, the cue ball will hit the 2. When shooting soft here, the cue ball will hit the 1.

## Reverse English

- Using reverse English is hitting the cue ball on the opposite side.

- This shot is more difficult to control than one in which you use natural English.

- Speed also affects the angle at which the cue ball rebounds off the cushion

- when applying reverse English.

- The harder you stroke, the wider the angle of the cue ball coming off the rail. With a hard hit the cue ball will contact the 2 ball. With a soft hit the cue ball will hit the 1 ball.

# ONE-RAIL SHOTS

## The most common bank or kick shot is the one-railer because it is the easiest one to learn

If you have to bank a ball, you should go only one rail unless the shot forces you to go more. One-rail banks and kicks come up in just about every game. It is an important part of the game that requires a good amount of practice.

The average player steps up to the table and shoots the bank shot with no real plan in mind. Bank-and-kick shots are tricky and need your full attention. If you are just starting out, you want to spend most of your time getting the stance and stroke down. Then you need to learn how to pocket balls and to control the cue ball. Learning the banks and kicks will come after you have been playing a while and feel comfortable with the other parts of your game.

### Cut Bank Shot

- Cut the ball to the right to bank it into the right corner pocket. As a result of the cut, the object ball will have left English.

- When you shoot the shot with medium speed and a center ball hit, the object ball will bank short, particularly if you are shooting into the natural angle.

- Use left English on the cue ball to negate the right English on the object ball, and it will bank more naturally.

### Cross Bank Shot

- A cross bank shot is used when the cue ball crosses the path of the object ball before it goes into the pocket.

- These banks are easy to judge as long as you don't shoot too hard.

- Because you are cutting the ball, the object ball will bank a little longer than the angle it goes into the cushion.

- Use a little right English on the cue ball or cut the 1 ball a little more.

When you start playing the game of 9-Ball, kicks and bank shots will appear more often. The reason is that in 9-Ball you have only one ball to hit, unlike 8-Ball, where you have seven high balls or seven low balls to shoot at. In 14.1, Straight Pool, you can shoot any ball on the table.

After you have played the game for a while, aiming for a bank shot will become natural for you. Top players rely on their instincts and feel for most shots.

Practice banks and kicks with simple setups. You may want to practice with friends by playing a game in which every shot has to be either banked or kicked in. Doing this will go a long way in improving your banking and kicking skills.

## Natural Angle Kick Shot

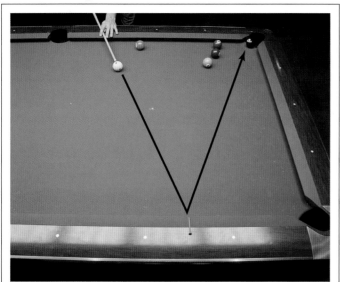

- This is a natural angle kick shot to make the 8 ball because your opponent's balls are blocking the direct path for a clean shot.

- Shoot into the cushion at one and a half diamonds to the right of the left corner pocket.

- Remember to use a center ball hit on the cue ball when shooting this shot.

- Even a small amount of English will cause you to miss.

## Reverse English Kick Shot

- This is a great example of where you need to use reverse English to win the game.

- You need to shoot out far enough to give you a direct path to the 8 ball.

- This can be achieved by applying left English on the cue ball.

- You also need to use a medium-speed stroke.

# TWO-RAIL SHOTS

## Learning the angles of the pool table will help you make the two-rail bank or kick shot

At times you need to kick or bank a ball off of two rails. Some of these shots are not as difficult as they sound. The easiest situation in which to use a two-rail kick occurs when you kick at a ball near a corner pocket. Most players have a natural feel for these shots.

Two-rail kicks are much easier than two-rail banks. On a two-rail kick shot, you strike only the cue ball and send it into the two rails. When you shoot a two-rail bank shot, the cue ball hits another ball, and then that ball goes two rails. A lot of things can change the path of the object ball when you hit the cue ball into it. If you have any English on the cue ball and hit into the object ball, you affect the path of the object ball.

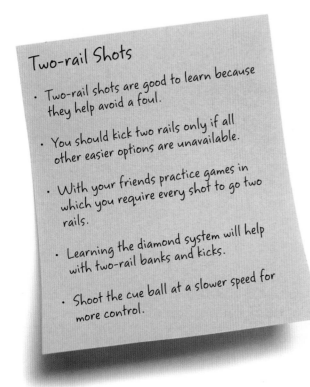

### Two-rail Shots

- Two-rail shots are good to learn because they help avoid a foul.

- You should kick two rails only if all other easier options are unavailable.

- With your friends practice games in which you require every shot to go two rails.

- Learning the diamond system will help with two-rail banks and kicks.

- Shoot the cue ball at a slower speed for more control.

*Two-rail Bank Shot*

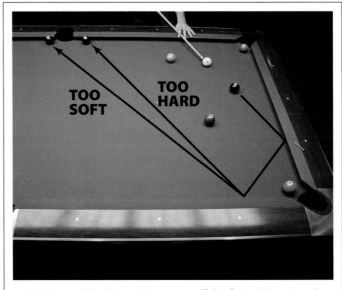

- This two-rail bank is easier than others because it's more natural and easier to judge.

- As in all other bank shots, speed plays a big role in this shot.

- If you shoot with too hard a stroke, it will bank short off the first rail, causing the 8 ball to miss short. If you shoot too soft, the 8 ball will miss long.

- Use a medium-speed stroke to pocket the 8 ball in the side. This shot also is easier to control.

When you kick with just the cue ball, you have to concentrate only on where you strike the cue ball and where to hit the rail. Banking requires doing both of these along with aiming at the object ball.

Center ball hits and correct speed help you to become more consistent with these shots. The softer you are able to hit the shot, the more control you have over it. The term table speed refers to the speed at which the cue ball reacts naturally. If you hit a ball too hard into a rail, it will come out short; if you hit it too soft, it will lengthen out and go long.

Table speed will allow the ball to take its natural path off the rail. Some players compare table speed with lag speed. The lag is the opening shot in which both players lag a ball up the table and back to see who comes closest to the end rail. Table speed is dependent on the length of the shot.

## Two-rail Bank Shot, Long Cushion First

- This is another two-cushion shot that comes in handy.

- Play the 1 ball into the long rail, and it will then hit the short rail and come back into the bottom right-hand corner.

- If you are playing 8-Ball, you would play this with a stop shot.

- As a one-pocket shot, play this with a little bit of draw so you don't leave your opponent a shot if you miss.

## Two-rail Kick Shot

- Knowing how to execute a two-rail kick shot is handy.

- It is especially handy when you try to make a hit on or pocket a ball where you have no chance for a one-rail kick.

- When stroked at the proper speed, the cue ball will rebound off the second rail and hit the 5 ball.

- This shot is much easier to judge and control when using natural English.

# THREE-RAIL SHOTS

## Three-rail banks and kicks are used more for a defensive play than offensive play

If you are not good at geometry and you want to shoot three-rail banks and kicks, you will need to get a book on the diamond system, which helps you sort through three-rail banks and kicks (see Additional Reading in the Resources for more information).

As with two-rail shots, kicking three rails is much easier than banking three rails. For the same reason, it is easier to hit the cue ball into a rail with control than it is to hit the cue ball into an object ball and then into a rail with control.

Three-rail banks and kicks are used on every shot in the game of Three-cushion billiards. Three rails are the minimum number of rails the ball has to travel to score a point. If you

### Three-rail Shots

- These shots are not used often, but they are handy to have in your tool box to help you win more games.

- Combine your creativity and the banking systems to execute multiple rail shots.

- These shots need to be executed with precision using the correct English and speed of stroke.

- You will be amazed at how much you can do with these shots and how many more options you will have once you learn these.

### Short Three-rail Bank

- This short three-rail bank into the side pocket is a good shot to practice from different locations.

- Start at the location you see here and then move the object ball closer to the long rail to find out the limits of making this shot.

- If you shoot this shot too hard, it will be difficult to judge.

- For instance, you may end up making the object ball in the corner pocket instead of the side.

want to improve this part of your game, try playing Three-cushion billiards.

When you face a three-rail shot, you should look at the last rail that needs to be hit. Try to figure out at what angle the cue ball needs to come off of that rail in order to make contact with your object ball. Then go to the second rail and look at the angle from there to the third rail. Finally, look at the first rail. It helps to dissect this shot from the object ball back to the cue ball.

Top players seem to have what is known as a "natural feel"

for a shot. They have played the game so many times and have seen every possible angle there is. So they rely on their natural instincts when shooting multiple rail banks or kicks. Most of the time top players shoot these shots as two-way shots. They try to pocket the ball, but, in case they miss it, they will leave their opponent without a shot.

## *Long Three-rail Kick*

- Here is a three-rail shot that comes up in 8-Ball.

- The object is to hit the long rail first, then the short rail, then the long rail again to pocket the 8 ball in the side.

- Shoot this shot with right-hand English for it to reverse off the short rail,

which will cause the cue ball to change directions.

- Practice this shot at different speeds to learn how much English to use, and you'll be prepared for the next time this occurs.

## *Three-rail Kick Using Running English*

- When shooting a three-rail kick, similar to a two-rail kick, it is much easier to control with running English than with a center ball hit or reverse English.

- In most three-rail kicks the more English you apply, the easier it is to judge.

- Try to keep your cue as level as possible and hit on the center axis of the cue ball.

- For this shot you should use left English and try to pocket the 8 ball.

# THE FIRST SHOT

## Depending on the game, the first shot approach could be different for each

The first shot is sometimes your most important one. The reason is that, as a game plays on, the most critical shots seem to be toward the end. But in many cases, the first shot can determine the outcome of the game.

For example, if you play 9-Ball, your strategy will be different than your strategy for 8-Ball or Straight Pool. In 9-Ball you need to hit the lowest-number ball on the table first. You want to either pocket that ball or play a safe. 8-Ball has much more decision making. You need to look at all the balls on the table. Taking a walk around the table gives you a good idea of which category of balls will give you a better chance at winning.

### Walk around the Table

- Study the table carefully before deciding on your first shot. Walk around the entire table.

- If you do not take the time to walk entirely around the table, you may miss an opportunity for a shot that you did not know existed.

- To become a better player, you need to make this walk part of your regular routine.

- It is not necessary to spend a great deal of time looking around; a quick check will be all that you need.

### Study the Table

- Study the table for run-out patterns and problem balls.

- Few players are able to run out the table (pocket all the balls and win the game), but you want to be able to make as many balls as possible.

- You need to study the table before each shot, not only after the break.

- If you notice that many of your balls are in difficult positions, you need to think of a good place for a safety shot.

In Straight Pool, however, you can shoot at any ball on the table, so your strategy will be different than in 9-Ball or 8-Ball. You look for a ball that can be used to break open the rack to keep the run going. If there isn't a ball that can be used to break the rack, then you look for a good safe, one by which you can move some balls out from the rack and still not allow your opponent a shot. Every game has a different strategy for the opening shot. The game determines the best option for you. And in other games, such as One Pocket, the strategy is different from the three games listed above.

## Recognize Problem Balls

Problem Balls

- Problem balls are ones that are difficult to pocket because of their location on the table or their location in a cluster of other balls.

- Balls that are frozen or close to the rails are also difficult to pocket and play position on.

- Learning to recognize the problem balls on the table will go a long way in winning games.

- In a game of 8-Ball, you want to choose the group that has fewer problem balls after the break.

## Choosing High or Low

Problem Balls

- You need to be able to make your first shot. If only one shot is available, this will take away any choices you have.

- In this photo the high balls are the better choice because the 2 and 7 are problem balls.

- Take the group that has fewer problem balls.

- Shooting the 14 ball will allow you to get easy position on the next shot.

# THINKING THREE BALLS AHEAD
## This strategy requires accurate cue ball control

Top players think three balls ahead when they play. But average players think about only the ball they are shooting and maybe one more. The better the player you are, the more you can control the cue ball and think further into the future of the game. To think three balls ahead, you must be able to control the path of the cue ball. It requires you to get to small areas so that you have the proper angle to have position for your next shot. Having the correct angle for each shot makes

running out the table that much easier. During the course of a game, most players will miss some of their position shots and have to make adjustments. It is rare that a player gets perfect position every time that he runs out.

The beginning-to-average player wants to make the ball he shoots at. After all, it will do him no good to get position if he doesn't pocket his object ball. You can still think ahead simply by looking for problem balls. Problem balls are the ones that

### Thinking Three Balls Ahead from the First Shot

- Here you want to shoot the 14 ball in the corner with a stop shot.

- Then hit the 15 ball in the corner and come around for the 11 ball into the same pocket the 14 went into.

- Draw back a little and pocket the 8 ball in the side.

- Mentally you have to always be thinking about where the cue ball needs to be and how you are going to get it there.

### Thinking Three Balls Ahead for Clusters

- At times the third ball ahead may be in a cluster of balls.

- You need to have a plan to break it out.

- By playing the 11 ball in the corner and hitting top English on the cue ball, you can break out the 14 ball.

- It is better to break out a ball earlier than later. If the ball rolls into an awkward position, you still have time to figure out another play for it.

are in clusters, are on a rail, or have no pocket that they can go into. You will have to play position for these balls, break them out, or play a safety. Having experience is the only way to determine the best method for you.

## Scenario for Thinking Three Balls Ahead

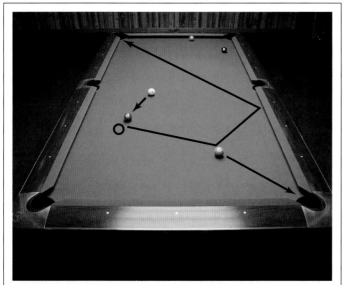

- Sometimes when thinking three balls ahead, you must move the cue ball from one end of the table to the other.

- Shoot the 3 ball in the corner and let the cue ball roll forward.

- You can play either a draw shot or a cut shot on the 4 ball to get position on the ball down table.

- There are always different ways to get there; take the one that you find the easiest.

## Thinking Three Balls Ahead for Defense

- At times you will have no option but to play a safe.

- You want to position yourself correctly so that you can make the safety play as easy as possible for yourself.

- Play a stop shot on the 2 ball and then a stop shot on the 3 ball.

- Doing this will give you a great angle to play a safety off the 4 ball and leave the cue ball behind the 8 ball.

# TARGET ZONES

## Stop your cue ball in intended areas to create makeable shot opportunities

Too many players neglect to look for a target area. This is the area the cue ball can roll into and leave you a shot. You do not always have to play perfect position to have a shot on the next ball. This situation will usually occur when multiple balls are on the table, although it does occur even when only one ball is left.

Target zones are much larger areas than most players realize. You must think ahead and look for these areas for best results. If you try to play into a tight spot and miss your position, you may not be able to get a good hit on your next shot, thereby committing a foul and possibly giving away the game. Look for the best angle to approach target areas. You

### Targeting Position Area, Scenario 1

- You are shooting at the 1 ball. Visualize a target area that will give you an angle to shoot the 2 ball and get a good leave on the 4 ball.

- Here you can strive for a big target area that will leave you in a good position.

- Remember to visualize a target area for each ball you shoot at.

- Doing this will give you a better chance of running out the rack.

### Targeting Position Area, Scenario 2

- You are shooting the 3 ball. The 4 ball is near the end rail and can go in only one pocket because the 6 is blocking a corner.

- Visualize a target area to position your cue ball on the correct side of the 4.

- From there you will be in a good spot to shoot in the 4 and have a leave on the 5.

- The 6 ball is a hanger, so look for your leave on the 7 ball.

want to give yourself as much room for error as possible.

Don't try to run the cue ball all the way around the table because most times this attempt will end in failure. Look for an area you can stop the cue ball in without having to jeopardize your shot or position. Sometimes it is better to swallow your medicine than to suffer the consequences. Playing smart will win you more games.

A target zone can be used for both playing position on your next shot or for playing a safety. For a defensive strategy, try placing the cue ball into a target zone to leave your opponent

no shot. After you have learned to recognize target zones, you will become a more consistent player. Remember that pool is a thinking game and that the smarter you play, the more you win.

## *Targeting Position Area, Scenario 3*

- Shoot the 2 ball into the side pocket. You can play it soft, or you can hit the cue ball with high English.

- If you use high English, you want to make sure the cue ball comes off the first rail and goes into the target zone.

- If you come up short, you may get stuck behind the 7 or 8 ball.

- This situation will leave you with a good shot on the 3 ball and easy position to make the 4.

## *Targeting Position Area, Scenario 4*

- Play position for three target zones.

- You want the best possible position for the 5 ball.

- You need your cue ball in target zone 2 for a shot on the 4 ball.

- Target zone 1 is the best spot for your cue ball to be. It will get you to target zone 2 after shooting the 3 ball. A stop shot on the 4 ball will get you to target zone 3 to make the 5 ball.

# KEEPING IT SIMPLE

## Playing by the KISS policy (Keep it simple, stupid) will win you games

Many games are lost because players try to do more than they are capable of. Keeping the game simple is the best way to go. If you are not good at hitting a draw shot, then you shouldn't try to draw the cue ball around the table. Realizing your own strengths and weaknesses will make you a better and smarter player.

Keeping things simple is as basic as it sounds; don't do something stupid that causes you to lose the game. It is far better to play a safe shot than to take a wild attempt at a shot that you have a low percentage of pocketing. When you are in a game-deciding situation, always think before you shoot. Ask yourself: Is this the best move I can make? What are my

### Using Natural Angles

- Sometimes it's better to use natural angles for positioning your next shot.

- Simply use a touch of left English on the 2 ball in the corner. The cue ball will come around naturally for position on the 3 ball.

- Keep it simple. Look for the easiest path that the cue ball can travel without getting into trouble.

- If you need to adjust this path, it can be easily done with more top, more draw, or more English.

### Using Center Ball Hits

- You are shooting at the 6 ball, which is your last ball before the 8.

- If you hit the cue ball above center, it will roll down table and leave you behind one of the high balls.

- Instead you should use a center ball hit to execute a stop shot.

- You will have a clear shot to pocket the 8 ball and win the game.

alternatives? Sometimes it is something simple, and you will need to recognize it. It may mean taking a scratch on purpose or pushing a ball close to another one to make it more difficult for your opponent to run out the table.

Keeping the game as simple as possible is almost always your best option. Do not try to make it more complicated than it already is. Looking for these options will quickly make you a better and smarter player.

The KISS theory is one of the best theories in pool. This theory could apply to more than just pool, of course. Whenever you are in a difficult situation, remember what those four letters stand for. It will help you out more often than you think.

### *Recognizing Easier Position Routes, Scenario 1*

- You are solids and have the 6 ball and the 8 ball left to win the game.

- The natural angle will bring your cue ball three rails for position on the 8.

- Doing this is risky because the cue ball may hit the 14 or 11 ball as it goes around the table.

- It is better to pocket the 6 with a little bit of right English. This way the cue ball has no obstacles blocking its path for position on the 8 ball.

### *Recognizing Easier Position Routes, Scenario 2*

- You could shoot the 1 ball, follow the natural angle, and get to the rail near the 2.

- The cue ball may end up hitting the 7 or 9 ball on the way around the table and leave you no shot.

- Weigh your options. It's better to pocket the 1 and get the cue to hit off the rail and roll back slightly.

- You then have an angle on the 2 ball to use for position on the 3.

# POSITIONING USING RAILS
## The rails can help you get proper position for your next shot

Rails can be a player's secret weapon in a game. Many players do not know much about using the rails. The rails are made of hard rubber and are covered with cloth. They react differently depending on humidity, type of rubber, and tension of the bolts that attached them.

If you usually play at home, you will become familiar with the way the rails on your table react. When you play somewhere else, you may find that the rails do not play the same.

You will need to adjust your game accordingly.

The rails can be used in many ways to get position. Look at some of the trick shots listed in this book; you will notice the different shots the rails can make happen. You can shoot the cue ball into a rail and make it jump over a cluster of balls. You can also shoot the cue ball into an object ball and have that ball jump in the air and go cross side even with balls in the way.

### Shooting with the Cue Ball on the Rail

- When the cue ball is on the rail, you can still make a shot.

- Aim the cue ball into the rail about one-half diamond down the table. Hit this shot with draw and use a medium punch stroke.

- The ball will compress into the rail and start down table.

- When the draw kicks in, the cue ball will shorten up and allow you to make the ball.

### Shooting with the Cue Ball into the Rail

- Again the rail can be used to your advantage. You need to aim the cue ball to hit the rail just before the blocker ball.

- You need to hit the cue ball at eleven o'clock.

- With a punch stroke, hit the cue ball firmly, about 70 percent of your breaking speed.

- The cue ball will hit the rail, go over the blocker balls, and pocket the 8 in the corner.

Learning how to use the rails will make it easier to get the cue ball around the table for position. When you apply English to the cue ball, the rail will affect its path. Reverse English slows a cue ball, whereas running English speeds it up. The harder you shoot a ball into a rail, the shorter back the ball will return. If you shoot a ball softly into a rail, it will run longer. This fact is good to remember when shooting bank shots either cross side or cross corner.

## *Both Balls on the Rail*

- One of the most difficult shots occurs when both the cue ball and the object ball are on the rail.

- To make this shot, you need to put right English on the cue ball and shoot softly.

- The English will keep the cue ball hugging the rail.

- Doing this will allow the cue ball to get a full hit on the object ball to go into the corner.

## *Positioning by Jumping the Cue Ball off the Rail*

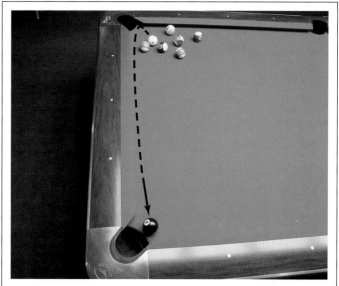

- At times it will look as if you have absolutely no shot.

- Because of the rails, you actually do have a shot here.

- You simply elevate the butt of the cue slightly and aim the tip just a hair above center.

- Hit with a punch stroke. The cue ball will hit the rail and jump over the blocker ball to pocket the object ball in the corner.

# SIZING UP YOUR OPPONENT

## Observing your opponent while playing helps you find his strengths and weaknesses

Figuring out which type of shots your opponent has trouble with goes a long way toward winning your match. Every player has a weakness in his game. It may be making long shots, executing banks, executing kicks, or even drawing the cue ball. By paying attention to these weaknesses, you may shoot a different shot because of the leave.

Some players have a reputation for being great at certain shots. After you play against the same person many times, you get to know all of them. You also get to know which shots he doesn't like.

Make observations about your opponents. Do they shy away from bank shots? Do they miss long shots? Are they

### Noting Opponents' Weaknesses

### Noting Opponents' Strengths

- Most players have problems with long shots. The more distance you can put between the cue ball and the object ball, the better chance your opponent has of missing.

- When you are not sure what to do, remember your opponent's weaknesses and play to them.

- When in doubt, playing a safety is always a good option no matter how good your opponent is.

- Pay attention to the entire game to make your shot decisions easier.

- If your opponent is a good bank shot player, try to leave him long shots. Whatever his strengths are, play away from them as much as you can.

- In this case play a stop shot with the cue ball while shooting it into the 9 ball.

- The cue ball will stop on the rail, and the 9 ball will go down to the opposite end of the table and sit on or near the short rail.

- Knowing your opponent will help you play smarter pool.

good at cutting a ball thin? By remembering these observations, you can make better judgments when playing safe. Don't play to their strengths; play to their weaknesses. Put your thinking cap on.

The players who win matches are the players who stay focused on the game. Pay attention to both sides of the game. You need a good defense as well as a good offense to win. No matter how good the other player is, if you can keep him seated, he cannot win. By knowing his strengths and weaknesses, you will have a better opportunity to do that.

## Two-way Shot

- Always think of ways to leave your opponent with a difficult shot.

- In the photo above, you want to play a two-way shot.

- Bank the 9 ball cross side and hit the cue ball with draw.

- If you miss the shot, chances are the cue ball will end up on the rail, and the 9 ball will be down the table, leaving your opponent with a long shot.

## Thin Cut Safety

- Here you want to cut the 9 ball thin on the left side.

- The 9 ball will stay on the rail and move toward the center of the rail.

- The cue ball will travel down to the far end of the table and end up on or near the opposite short rail.

- This situation will leave your opponent with a difficult shot or force him to play a safety.

# OFFENSE OR DEFENSE?

## Practice your defense as much as offense and watch your wins start to add up

To be successful in any sport, you need to be good both offensively and defensively. Pool is no different. To become a complete player, you need to work on both of these aspects of the game. Most beginners neglect their defensive strategies. Everyone wants to pocket balls and run out every time they get to the table. This strategy would work great if you never ran into problem balls or clusters and if every ball was hanging in front of a pocket. However, knowing when to put the stop sign up and play a safety will go a long way toward making you a smarter and more successful player.

Have you noticed that in almost every other sport, defense plays a huge part in winning? Basketball, football, and

### Risk versus Reward, Part 1

- Many games are won or lost on the first shot.

- Your first shot does not have to be offensive; many times the better move is to play defense.

- When you are left with only one shot and no way to get to your next one, you need to think defense.

- In this situation, there is no easy way to get good position on the 2 ball. The smart move is to play safe. The next photo shows the results of the safety.

### Risk versus Reward, Part 2

- Knowing when to choose between an offensive shot and a defensive one can make the difference between winning and losing.

- In this case by simply playing the 1 ball into the rail and rolling the cue ball forward onto the 3 ball, you have locked up your opponent.

- The position to get to the 2 ball was much riskier and more difficult than playing the safe.

- You weigh the risk/reward factor mostly when you are left with a difficult shot.

baseball are three examples. Teams do not win champion-ships unless they have a great defense. Pool is no different. If you cannot play a good defensive game, you will have a difficult time winning. Work just as hard on defense as you do on offense. You will be amazed at how many more games you win. Good defense has a number of benefits: It frustrates your opponent and wears him down. It gives you more ball-in-hand situations. And, if your opponent is able to make a good hit, it gives you a good chance at still making the ball.

You can use many practice drills to work on your defense.

For instance, play a game with your buddies in which you attempt to make the other player table or pocket scratch three times in a row. The more attention you give to specific skill sets in practice, the better you'll be when it's game time.

## Two-way Shots, Part 1

- At times you will have what is known as a "two-way shot."

- This means that you have the opportunity to pocket your ball, but that if you miss, you will leave your opponent with no shot.

- In this situation you have the opportunity to bank the 1 ball cross corner. Hit the cue ball with draw.

- If you pocket the 1 ball, you will have an easy shot for the 2 ball in the side pocket.

## Two-way Shot Safe, Part 2

- As you can see in this photo, the 1 ball has been missed on the cross corner bank.

- By drawing the cue ball back, you have locked your opponent up on the 9 ball.

- This situation gives you a good chance at getting ball-in-hand.

- This is why looking at all your options before shooting is important.

# RECOGNIZING OPTIONS

## Learn to identify opportunities on the table that could give you the advantage

Being able to recognize the best option goes a long way toward winning your match. For some players it is just a natural instinct. They look at the balls quickly and start shooting. The best method is to study the table. You need to visualize your best option, trying as much as possible to think three shots ahead. If you are playing 8-Ball, you start out by looking

for clusters. If more low balls are clustered together, then you probably want to take the high balls. If the clusters look about the same for each group, you can check to see which category of balls has more open pockets to shoot at. Are there more balls closer to the pockets in one of the categories than the other? Is there a chance that you could pocket

*Analyzing the Table*

- As mentioned, analyzing the table after the break and before each shot is critical.

- Depending on the game you are playing, the first shot may be different.

- Some games such as 8-Ball and 7-Ball are more of an offensive game than a game of One Pocket.

- The type of game and the objective of that game will inform your decision.

*Run Out or Play Safe?*

- Do you go for the runout or play for a safety?

- Playing the 1 ball in the side pocket and running the cue ball four rails for position is a risky shot.

- Blocker balls could get you into trouble. It would be

better to play the 1 ball in the side pocket softly and leave yourself a shot on the 2.

- Bank the 2 up table and leave the cue ball behind the 5.

76

the 8 ball out of turn because one category of balls has the 8 ball blocking its pocket?

Your mind will have to run through this checklist and more in order to make the correct decision. If you are playing 9-Ball, can you make the 1 and get position on the 2 ball? If you can't, where can you leave your opponent with no shot? What are the trouble balls? Will you be able to play for them in a pocket, or will they need to be broken out? Anytime you have to break balls out of clusters, position is much more difficult.

As you see, many factors determine your options. You can't remember everything, but experience and practice will help you make the correct choice. Go with the one that you feel most comfortable with. Your first choice is usually your right choice.

## *Playing Safe for Ball-in-hand, Part 1*

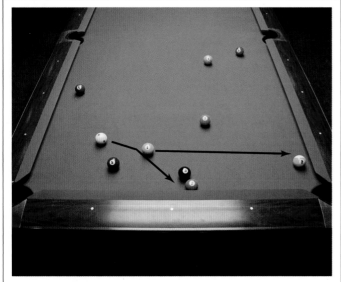

- When the opportunity presents itself to get ball in hand, you want to take advantage of it.

- In this situation you want to shoot the 1 ball behind the 9 ball.

- You want to have the cue ball roll up behind the 7 and 8 balls.

- The closer you can get the cue ball onto a blocker ball, the better your safety will be.

## *Playing Safe for Ball-in-hand, Part 2*

- The result of the safety played in the photo to the left leaves your opponent with few options.

- For your opponent to get a good hit on the 1 ball, he will have to make a good kick shot.

- With all of the obstacles in the way, there is a good chance of a foul.

- If you do get ball-in-hand, you can play an easy 1-9 combination shot.

# TWO-WAY SHOTS

These are probably the best shots you can use in the games of 8-Ball and 9-Ball

Pool is a thinking man's game. Many games are won or lost because of decision making. If you have knowledge going into a game, you greatly increase your chances of winning. You need to be aware of everything that is happening on the table. A carom shot or a combination may be possible to win the game. If you're not thinking clearly, you may miss this opportunity. When the opportunity for a two-way shot comes up, it is a wise choice to play it. A two-way shot is one in which the shooter plays offense and defense at the same time. He elects to make a run at the shot but knows that if he misses he will leave his opponent safe.

Look for such a shot when you play. It will usually occur

*Two-way Shots, Scenario 1*

- For this shot you want to cut the 1 ball in the corner pocket.

- It is a thin cut, and the shot can easily be missed.

- If you make the 1 ball in the corner, the cue ball will roll down table for position on the 2 ball.

- If you miss the 1 ball, the 1 ball will sit near the corner pocket, and the cue ball will roll down table and leave your opponent no shot.

*Two-way Shots, Scenario 2*

- In a game of 9 ball, you want to shoot the 3 ball cross side.

- Hit the cue ball with a draw stroke.

- If you make the 3 ball, you have position on the 4 in the corner pocket.

- If you miss the 3 ball, the cue ball will draw back behind the 5 and 7 balls, leaving your opponent no shot.

when you have a shot that you are not confident in. In other words, you have about as much chance of missing it as you do of making it.

Be sure to leave yourself a shot on the following ball in case you do make the first shot. The two-way shot is one of the best plays, especially in 9-Ball. In this game your opponent has only one ball to shoot at. So, this type of situation will come up more often. Walking around the table when you have a difficult shot will help you find a good solution. This tactic works in 8-Ball as well. Even though your opponent has more balls to shoot at, you may be able to leave him safe if he misses. This is especially true at the end of the game when fewer balls are on the table.

## Two-way Shots, Scenario 3

- This is another good example of a two-way shot for the game of 9-Ball. Shoot the 3 ball up the rail into the corner pocket.

- Hit bottom right English on the cue ball.

- If you make the 3 ball, the cue ball will be in perfect position for the 4.

- If you miss the 3 ball, the cue ball will be behind the 5, 6, and 7 balls, leaving your opponent with a kick shot.

## Two-way Shots, Scenario 4

- Playing 9-Ball, you would cut the 2 ball in the side pocket.

- Hitting the cue ball firmly with low left English will bring it back two rails and in position for the 3 ball.

- If you miss, the cue ball will be on the bottom rail, and the 2 ball will be on the short rail at the other end of the table.

- The 4, 5, and 7 balls will block out any chance for an open shot.

# STITCH SAFETIES

## The best safety is when you leave your opponent no chance of making a good hit

Stitch safeties are ones in which you lock up your opponent so that he has a difficult time making a good hit on the ball. These are the best safeties to play. If you can force your opponent to go two or more rails to make a good hit, you can increase your chances of getting ball-in-hand.

The best way to get a stitch safety is to freeze the cue ball to

a blocker ball. This situation will take away many of the angles for the shooter. It will force him either to shoot with English on the cue ball or go extra rails. Freezing the cue ball also takes away the possibility of shooting a jumpshot.

The easiest way to get a stitch safety is usually to hit a stop shot in which you replace the object ball with the cue ball.

*Stitch Safety Using a Blocker Ball*

- This is a great safety. Your opponent has no easy path to make a hit on the 1 ball.

- Anytime you can make your opponent go two or more rails for a good hit, you have a great chance of getting ball-in-hand because the percentage rate of making the hit drops.

- If your opponent makes a good hit, chances are you will have a shot on the 1 ball.

- When playing safe, you want to take away as many options from your opponent as possible.

*Stitch Safety with Stop Shot*

- The stop shot is one of the easiest safeties to play.

- Shoot straight into the 1 ball and stop the cue ball.

- The cue ball will freeze on the 2 ball, and the 1 ball will go to the other side of the table.

- Your opponent will be left with few options to make a legal hit on the 1 ball.

Stopping it dead where the other ball was will guarantee you a great safe. So, practice your stop shots. They will come in handy, especially for these types of situations.

You can play other types of stitch safeties. Rolling the cue ball forward with follow or using draw to lock up the cue ball is also effective. Your main objective is to give your opponent as few options as possible. You want to have every opportunity to get ball-in-hand. The player who has ball-in-hand controls the game in most cases. Take advantage of this option.

Practice stitch safeties as part of your regular routine. After you learn how to lock up your opponent, you will win many more games.

## Stitch Safety with Follow

- By using top or follow on the cue ball, you can play a safety here.

- Hit the cue ball with top English and have it roll forward and freeze on the 4 ball.

- Doing this will take out almost all angles for your opponent to get a good hit.

- With all safeties, take your time and think about where you want to leave the cue ball.

## Stitch Safety with Thin Cut

- When using a thin hit on the object ball, remember to shoot softly.

- Here you want to hit the 1 ball on the right side and put it behind the 6 ball.

- The cue ball will roll up to the other end of the table.

- You have forced your opponent to shoot a long, difficult kick shot in order to get a good hit.

# DEFENSE ON THE RAIL

## Use the rail as another form of defense; it takes away many options from your opponent

The rail can be your ally when playing defense. When you leave your opponent on the rail, you have taken a large portion of the table away from him, which means fewer options for him.

Remember that a pool table is a small surface and that the more you can do to make it difficult for your opponent, the

better your chances of winning. Often the little factors that many players don't think of make the difference between winning and losing. The rail may not seem like a huge disadvantage, but it can be detrimental to your opponent.

When the cue ball is up against the rail, your opponent will hit a small section on the cue ball. Doing this could cause a

### Defense with the Cue Ball on the Rail

- Leaving the cue ball on the rail makes the shot much more difficult.

- Also, when the cue ball is on the rail, only a limited amount of English can be applied.

- The 1 ball in the photo is a much tougher shot because of the cue ball position.

- If you cannot find a good safety behind a blocker ball, sometimes just leaving the cue ball on the rail works almost as well.

### Defense with Stop Shot Leaving Cue at Rail

- In a game of 9-Ball, this shot works as a good safe for two reasons.

- By hitting a stop shot, the cue ball will freeze to the rail.

- Also, the 1 ball will be blocked out by the 2 ball. This situation forces your

opponent to attempt a kick shot with the cue ball frozen to the rail.

- Because the cue ball is frozen, your opponent has a difficult time controlling the cue ball.

miscue. Also, the rail makes it difficult to play any type of English on the cue ball with control. The opponent will usually have to jack his cue up to apply English. Every time a player jacks up his cue, the chances for a miss increase.

So, the next time you have exhausted every option, think about leaving the cue ball on the rail. Doing so will not always work, but it will certainly make your opponent's next shot more difficult.

If you find yourself shooting from the rail, try not to do much with the cue ball. Keep your cue stick as level as possible. Keep your head still and stay down on the shot. Follow through with a smooth stroke on the ball. It is a difficult shot, but if you play the shot nice and easy, you will increase your chances of making it.

## *Defense with Follow Bringing Cue to Rail*

- Apply follow to the cue ball and bank the 1 ball up to the far end of the table.

- The cue ball will roll forward and freeze to the long rail.

- The 1 ball will be blocked out by the 2 ball along with the 3, 6, and 7 balls.

- You need to control the speed, and this will be a great safe to play.

## *Defense Tying Up Object Balls*

- At times no matter what you try, you cannot get a good hit.

- When you find yourself in this situation, don't just try a wild shot.

- Shoot the 8 ball softly so that it sits next to the 2 ball and ties them up.

- Doing this is a much better option than going for an unmakeable hit. Your opponent will now have to work around two clusters of balls to run out.

# TIPS & STRATEGIES

## Thinking all the time will keep your head in the game and keep you prepared for your turn

Pool is as much a mental game as it is a skill game. Less-skilled players can beat better players by outthinking them. The previous section on sizing up your opponent (see page 72) will be of great help in that department. If you can outthink opponents by playing safeties or leaving them bad options, you increase your chance of winning.

You cannot lose the game if you keep your opponent seated (unless, of course, you scratch on the 8 ball or knock it into the wrong pocket). The longer he is seated, the better your odds. This is why it is important to become a great defensive as well as offensive player.

Always think confidently. Sit up straight and don't show

### *Breaking Out Clusters*

- The correct shot here is to play the 1 ball into the left side of the 5 ball.

- Play a stop shot on the cue ball so that it remains behind the 8 ball.

- The cluster will break open, and the 1 ball will go to the opposite end of the table.

- Your opponent will be left with a kick shot. If he misses, you get ball-in-hand, and all the balls will be spread apart.

### *Playing Safe with Ball-in-hand*

- When you have ball-in-hand, at times you have no shot.

- You need to figure out a good safety to play.

- In some 9-Ball games, if the opponent scratches three times in a row, you win. You should take this into con-

sideration if your opponent is on his second scratch.

- Look for a place that you can best lock up either the cue ball or the object ball.

emotion when you miss. Showing emotion will only increase your opponent's confidence. Play your game. At times you may have to take an intentional scratch. At other times, in a game of 9-Ball, for example, you may have to shoot the 9 ball in early so it is not left in front of a pocket for your opponent to make.

Pool is a game of concentration. Most players miss shots because of lack of concentration more than anything else. Never take a shot for granted. The day you do, you will miss it.

Beware of drinking too much coffee before a match. The caffeine may give you the jitters. You want to be calm and relaxed. Exercise in the morning before you play. Stretching out before a match will help you feel more limber. The looser you feel at the table, the better you will play. Also try to keep a clear mind. Doing this can be difficult because there are always distractions. The less you think about during your game (outside of the game), the better you will play.

## Intentionally Knocking in the 9 Ball

- In this situation getting a good hit on the 1 ball would be difficult.

- If you go for the 1 ball and miss, your opponent would get ball-in-hand.

- He would then play the 1-9 combination shot for the win.

- Shoot the 9 into the corner. The 9 ball is then spotted, and your opponent has ball-in-hand. Now your opponent will be forced to run out all the balls instead of having an easy combination.

## Safeties

- Play the 1 ball into the 4 ball for a safety.

- Put top English on the cue ball and have it roll toward the 3 and 7 balls.

- You have the option of playing the 1-4 combination shot, but it is a difficult shot. If you do make the combination, you may not have a leave on the 1 ball.

- The smarter play here is the safety.

# BASIC RULES

## Here are essentials you need to know to play this game

8-Ball is one of the most popular games of pool. It is the easiest game to learn and play with friends and family. Even people who have not picked up a cue before will enjoy the game. A standard set of rules is used as a guide to play. However, a few variations on these rules exist, depending on whether you play at home, in bars, or in a league. Before you pick up your cue, remember to familiarize yourself with the rules that you and your opponent will use.

In leagues the person breaking is determined by the flip of a coin or a lag. After play has begun, whoever wins the game breaks the balls for the next game. When playing with more than two players, normally the winner stays on the table, and opponents rotate in to play. The incoming opponent will rack the balls for the breaking player.

After the rack is legally broken, play begins with players shooting at either stripes or solids. A player must clear his

### 8-Ball Rules

- One player shoots at stripes, and the other player shoots at solids.

- Your category is determined by sinking a ball on the break or making the first ball after the break.

- Fouls result in ball-in-hand for the other player.

- Win the game by pocketing the 8 ball in a legally marked or called pocket.

- The winner breaks the next rack, and play continues.

*The 8-Ball Rack*

- Rack all fifteen balls on the foot spot opposite the end you will break from.

- Place the 8 ball in the middle. The rest of the balls can be placed in any order. Many players put a solid in one back corner and a stripe in the other.

- The lead ball should be centered on the spot.

- Make sure the balls are racked together as tightly as possible without spaces between them so they will spread apart after the break.

category of balls before he can shoot at the 8 ball. The 8 ball must be made in a called or marked pocket to win the game.

To legally pocket a ball in 8-Ball, you must hit one of your category of balls first. If any balls of your category go in, you continue to shoot. This is much the same as in 9-Ball, where if you hit your object ball, anything that goes in counts. Some players play "call pocket" in which you must call every shot.

Sometimes during a game a player will attempt a shot and miss his ball completely or "scratch." When this happens the opponent will have ball-in-hand. The opponent can put the cue ball anywhere on the table and shoot from there. The only time the player has to shoot from behind the head string is when the player scratches on the break. The head string is the imaginary line that runs across the table at the second diamonds from the end of the table that the players break from.

## How to Win in 8-Ball

- You can win in several ways in 8-Ball in addition to sinking the 8 ball on the break.

- After you pocket all the balls in your category, you need to sink the 8 ball in a legally marked or called pocket.

- You may not pocket the 8 ball at the same time as the last ball in your category.

- If your opponent fouls by knocking the 8 ball in early or scratching while shooting on the 8, you win the game.

### 8-Ball Rules, Fouls

Sometimes a player will foul during the course of a game. There are several ways a foul may occur:

- Failure to strike your category of balls first

- Failure to hit a rail after contacting your object ball

- Scratching the cue ball in a pocket or on the floor

- Accidentally touching the cue ball before or during a shot

# BEFORE & AFTER BREAKING
## Be ready for developments before and after the break

Breaking the rack is not about only spreading the balls apart. Several factors, such as how the balls are racked, can affect the break. After the balls are broken, the results of the break will determine what happens next.

Most of the time an opponent racks the balls for the breaking player. To be a good rack, the balls should be put together as tightly as possible. The balls should be centered with the lead ball placed on the spot.

Before play can continue, the rack must be legally broken. If the rack is not legally broken, then the balls are re-racked and broken by the same player. If an illegal break results in a scratch, the balls are re-racked and broken by the opposite player. Depending on the league or tournament you play in, these rules may be different.

When the breaking player makes balls on the break, he continues his turn. The category of balls you make on the break

### Before the Break

- It is a good idea to check the rack from time to time. Your opponent will be more likely to give you a good rack if you check it.

- Decide where you want to break, which can be from anywhere behind the line at the second diamond.

- You should place the cue ball closer to the line to get the most power from your break.

- Most players place the cue ball to either side instead of straight on with the rack.

### Legal Break

- A legal break occurs when four object balls hit a rail after you strike the rack.

- When an object ball goes into a pocket, the break is legal no matter how many balls hit a rail.

- Break as hard as you can with control. The balls should be scattered across the table with few clusters.

- Soft breaking, or breaking just hard enough to get four balls to a rail, is usually not allowed.

is what you shoot at for the rest of the rack. If you make both stripes and solids, no matter how many of each, then you still have your choice of balls to shoot at. Some rules give you a choice of ball no matter what goes into the pocket. When no object balls go into a pocket, your turn is over, and the opponent has the choice.

Choosing your first shot after the break can make or break your game. Look at the table layout after the break. Here are some questions you want to consider: How many problem balls are in each category? Are problem balls positioned well for better defense opportunities? Can I break out the clusters? If there are no clusters, determine which category of balls is easier for you to run out.

## After the Break

- After breaking the balls, one ball of each category goes into a pocket.

- You have open table with the balls spread out as pictured.

- There is one cluster of stripes. If you choose stripes, you will be forced to break those out to complete a run.

- All the solids are free of clusters. You should choose solids because you will be more likely to run out.

## Choosing the First Shot

- Now that you have selected your category, you need to choose your first shot.

- You should consider shooting a high-percentage shot to secure your category choice.

- Visualize a pattern that would give you the best chances of running the table.

- In this layout the best choice is the 1 ball in the corner. This shot is both a makeable shot and a good setup ball for positioning your run.

# BREAKING
## Breaking is an important aspect of the game and gives you a competitive edge

A good break can give you an advantage over your opponent. Many players strive to make balls on the break so they can take control of the table. Making a ball on the break may also be the start of a break and run.

It is possible to win the game on the break when you make the 8 ball on the break without scratching. However, if you make the 8 on the break, and the cue ball scratches, then you lose the game. So you want to be careful when trying out this break.

Although it's possible to make an 8 on the break from multiple breaking positions, you will increase your chances when you use the position most recommended by the pros.

### Break Position for 8 on the Break

- You will impress your friends and win more games if you can make an 8 ball on the break.

- The best position to make the 8 on the break is with the cue ball about one ball away from either of the side rails.

- Bridge your hand on the side rail for more stability in your stroke.

- Place the cue ball within a comfortable distance near the second diamond.

### Cue Ball Contact Point for 8 on the Break

- Aim for a full hit on the second ball while just barely missing the lead ball.

- Use low inside English on the cue ball to avoid a scratch.

- If you hit the ball too thin or without English on the cue ball, you may scratch.

- Practice this break for best results. The balls will spread out nicely, and your chances of making an 8 ball on the break will increase.

You can use several positions from which to break. You should try out different positions to find your comfort zone. You also want to optimize your chances to make balls on the break.

Professional players rarely break from straight on with the rack. The cue ball is often placed to either side of the center anywhere from ½ to 1½ diamonds over. The breaking area often referred to as "the kitchen" is from behind an imaginary line that goes across the table from the second diamond up. The cue ball will have more momentum striking the rack if you place it closer to that line.

## Common Break Position

- A good break makes the balls scatter apart as much as possible. When the cue ball is closer to the rack, it will strike with more speed.

- Place the cue ball near the line at the second diamond up and about one-half diamond to either side of the center.

- Bridge your hand on the table behind the cue ball.

- Try breaking from different positions to find out where you get the best results.

## Cue Ball Contact Point on Common Break

- When breaking near the middle of the table, you should aim for a full hit on the head ball in the rack and use a center ball hit on the cue ball.

- Doing this will transfer more energy into the rack, causing the balls to spread out more.

- Remember to follow through on your break. Your chances of making a ball on the break will increase.

- Doing this will also give you an opportunity to get a good run after the break.

8-BALL

# PATTERNS IN 8-BALL
## Optimize your chances to make more balls during your turn

When you play 8-Ball, you play patterns without even realizing it. Players of all skill levels try to make a ball and also have a leave to pocket the next ball. This strategy is the beginning stages of pattern play. How far you go with it is entirely up to you. Many players enjoy pool, whether they dream of becoming a break-and-run player or just want to have a fun night out with friends.

You can string balls together whether you visualize an entire table or think only three balls ahead. Many players think three balls ahead and adjust their sequence for the next three balls after they make a ball in. When choosing a pattern, it is a good idea to work backward from the last ball for the best position route.

Playing patterns in 8-Ball is like putting together the pieces of a puzzle. If you get out of position, you will need to look at your options very closely. You may have to play a safe or take

*Patterns, Scenario 1*

- In this example the 7 ball in the side will be your last shot before shooting the 8 ball. So, you want to position yourself for that shot.

- Make the 1 ball first. Doing this will give you a good angle on the 3 ball.

- Make the 3 ball to set up for the 7 ball in the side.

- You will be in a good position for your shot on the 8 ball.

*Patterns, Scenario 2*

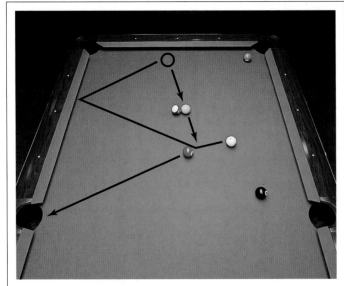

- Here you are solids, and your opponent is stripes.

- You do not have an easy run because the 1 ball is tied up.

- Taking the 3 ball first gives you a good angle for the breakout, or you have the option of playing position on the 1 ball in the lower right corner.

- If you do not have a shot on the 1 ball, you still have the 7 ball to shoot at for positioning on the 1.

a chance and shoot at a low-percentage shot.

When there are clusters you want to look for ways to break them out. You should consider breaking them apart as early as possible. If other balls are near the clusters, you can use them as breakout balls. You may want to leave another ball available in case you do not get a good shot from the balls you break out. If you find yourself stuck, you can plan to use defense. When you know you can't get a three-ball run, you want to make it more difficult for your opponent. You still want to put your cue ball in a good position to play safe.

## Patterns, Scenario 3

- First pocket the 5 ball with draw to play position on the 1 ball.

- Then you would shoot the 1 ball in the corner with draw and play position for the 3 ball in the corner or the side.

- Make the 3 ball and play position for the 7 ball in the side or corner.

- Then draw the cue ball back to set up for the 8 ball in the side pocket.

## Patterns, Scenario 4

- You are solids, and your opponent is stripes.

- The 2 ball is easy to make, but doing so won't give you good position on the 1 ball.

- Make the 1 ball first so your cue ball comes back to the center of the table.

- Then make the 2 ball in the side, and you will have a shot at the 8 ball in the corner.

# TIPS & STRATEGIES

## Whether you are a lower- or higher-skilled player, you can win by playing smart

Smart play is essential to the game. It's about not only your performance but also about making it as difficult as possible for your opponent to win. You can use different strategies depending on whether you are a lower- or higher-skilled player.

If you are new to the game or are a lower-skilled player,

the most important aspect to concentrate on is making your shots. You will not make balls all the time, but you will increase your chances by going for the simpler ones. If you are not sure whether you can make a ball, consider moving it near the pocket if you miss. It's even better to do this when you are blocking your opponent's ball. Doing this may

### Offense Strategies for Lower Skill Levels

- You are shooting at solids. It is important to make your first shot, so look for something easy.

- You should choose the 4 ball first and then shoot down table for the 1 ball.

- Save the 3 ball for last because it's blocking your opponent from shooting in the side pocket unless you have no other options.

- Make as many balls as you can. If you miss, you will leave your opponent long with one pocket blocked.

### Offense Strategies for Higher Skill Levels

- You are shooting at stripes. It is important that you choose a pattern that makes it easiest for you to run out.

- Remove any problem balls first so the rest of your shots are open.

- You should choose the 9 ball first because the 3 ball is blocking the side pocket, and you have an opportunity to make it in the corner.

- Doing this makes it easier for you to run the table out.

prevent your opponent from getting all his in before you do.

If you are a higher-skilled player, you are likely to make more balls and run out when you have an open table. It is important to know your ability so you take higher-percentage shots or play safe when you don't have a run. Sometimes it's better to play safe even when you have a shot.

Use problem balls to your advantage; when you can't break them out, consider playing a safe. Separate them while also not leaving your opponent a shot.

When an opponent runs balls, you have an opportunity either to run out or to play defense because you have a lot of balls to hide the cue behind. This is a good strategy if you can't run out on your first turn. The idea is to get your opponent to kick at a ball and increase your chance of getting ball-in-hand. Do that as many times as you need to clear the table and win the rack.

## Defense Strategies for Lower Skill Levels

- You are shooting at solids, and your opponent is on the 8 ball.

- You know you can't run out, and you don't want to leave your opponent a shot.

- Shoot very softly and pocket the 6 ball in the corner.

- Shoot straight into the 1 ball just enough for it to touch the rail. The cue ball should land just behind the 4 ball to increase your chances of getting ball-in-hand.

## Defense Strategies for Higher Skill Levels

- You are shooting at solids, and your opponent is shooting at stripes.

- You can't run out, and you want to make it as difficult as possible for your opponent.

- Shoot off the right side of the 2 ball just enough to block the pocket in front of the 10 ball.

- The cue ball will go down the opposite end of the table. Your opponent will be forced to play safe back.

# TABLE SIZE MATTERS

## Playing on different-size tables has its pros and cons

If you grew up playing in a pool room, chances are you played mostly on 9-foot tables. If you had a table at home, it would most likely be an 8-foot table. If you played at a bar, it would probably be a 7-foot table. Each table size has its advantages and disadvantages. The 9-foot table is longer and has tighter pockets. The professionals prefer this table when playing in a tournament. The tougher the conditions are, the better their chances against a weaker opponent. If the table is playing easy, the lesser-skilled player would have a better chance of winning against someone better than himself.

The 8-foot table, which is mostly found in homes, is what some like to call "the compromise." It is larger than the 7-foot and smaller than the 9-foot professional table. Price and space are usually the determining factors when someone buys the 8-foot table.

The 7-foot table, or the bar box table, is the smallest of

### 7-foot Tables

### 8-foot Tables

- Seven-foot tables are 3½ feet wide. They are popular in barrooms because of their size.

- They are much easier to move around and usually have one-piece slate, which is much easier to level.

- Barrooms also like 7-foot tables because of the coin-operating mechanism often found on them.

- Having coin-operated tables eliminates the need to have a counterperson to hand out balls and track table time.

- Eight-foot tables are the most popular size for home use.

- Because of limited room size, homeowners have found this size to be their best choice.

- Some 8-foot coin-operated tables are found in bars, but they are not common.

- Eight-foot tables have three pieces of slate, which make them harder to assemble. But they usually play better than 7-foot tables.

regulation-size tables. Usually it is found in bars or clubs. These tables are built to take abuse. They have four legs with levelers making them simple to adjust.

Whichever table size you choose, you still have to make the ball into the pocket. The large 9-foot table gives you more room to move the cue ball around, but you have longer shots into tighter pockets. The 8-foot table is in the middle. Your shots are shorter than on the 9-footer, but the pockets most likely are larger. The 7-foot table makes for shorter shots with larger pockets, but you have less room to work with.

## 9-foot Tables

- Professionals play most of their tournaments on 9-foot tables.

- The actual playing surface is 50 by 100 inches. The tables have three pieces of slate.

- The 9-foot table is commonly found in pool and billiard rooms.

- You need professional installers to set up this table. They have the tools and experience to level this table.

### Playing on Different-size Tables

Playing on different-size tables has pros and cons:

- Angles are different and are in proportion with the size of the table.

- You should use a softer stroke for a 7-foot table than you would for a 9-foot table.

- Balls are closer together on a 7-foot, causing more congestion.

- Long shots are easier on a 7-foot table because there is less distance between the balls and the pockets than on a 9-foot table.

- Pockets are usually larger on a 7-foot table.

# BASIC RULES
## Learn these simple 9-Ball rules, and you will be ready to play a game

9-Ball is a rotation game that requires more skillful position play than 8-Ball. The main reason is because you are shooting at only one ball because you must shoot them in order. Many top players prefer to play 9-Ball over other games.

Regardless, players of all levels can still enjoy a good game of 9-Ball with their friends or in leagues. Many leagues have 9-Ball teams as well as 8-Ball teams. 9-Ball has several sets of rules; the following are the most common.

As in 8-Ball, the breaking player is determined by a flip of a coin or a lag. Then whoever wins the rack breaks it. The other person or incoming opponent racks the balls.

After the rack is legally broken, play begins by shooting from the lowest-numbered ball on the table to the highest. When you make the 9 ball, you win the rack. The 9 can be pocketed early with a combination shot or shot in last after all the balls have been cleared. Some players call the 9 ball,

### 9-Ball Rules

- Shoot the balls in numerical order.

- Fouls result in ball-in-hand anywhere on the table for the other player.

- Win the game by pocketing the 9 ball legally at anytime during the game.

- The winner breaks the next rack, and play continues.

*The 9-Ball Rack*

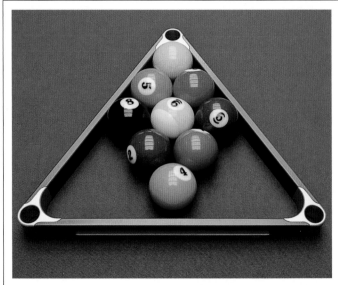

- Rack the 1 to 9 balls on the foot spot opposite the end you will break from.

- Place the 1 ball in the front and the 9 ball in the middle. The rest of the balls can be placed in any order.

- The 1 ball should be centered on the spot.

- The balls should be racked together as tightly as possible without spaces between them so they will break apart well.

but doing so is not required. If a player pockets the 9 ball on the break, he wins the game. If he pockets the 9 ball on the break and scratches, the 9 ball is spotted, and the opposing player has ball-in-hand anywhere on the table. When a player fouls during a 9-Ball game, the opponent will have ball-in-hand from anywhere on the table.

## *How to Win in 9-Ball*

- You can win in 9-Ball in several ways in addition to sinking the 9 on the break.

- You must pocket all the balls in numerical order and then sink the 9 ball last.

- You may pocket the 9 ball early in the rack by using a legal combination or carom shot to knock it in.

- In this photo you can play the 3 ball into the 9 ball for the win.

**9-Ball Fouls**

You can foul in several ways in 9-Ball:

- When you do not hit the lowest-numbered ball first

- When you do not hit a rail after contacting the object ball

- When you scratch the cue ball in a pocket or on the floor

- When you accidentally touch the cue ball before or during a shot

**9-BALL**

99

# RACKING
## A good rack will improve your chances to make balls on the break

The balls numbered 1 through 9 are racked in a diamond shape. You can use either a diamond-shaped rack made for nine balls or the most common rack, the triangular one. The 1 ball must be in the front, the 9 must be in the middle. The rest of the balls can be in any order. Many players choose to put the 3 and 5 balls behind the 1 ball and the 2 and 4 balls in the second-to-last row. On the break these balls will often spread to opposite ends of the table and make a more difficult run. This is a good strategy when you play an opponent who can run out on you.

To be a good rack, the balls must have as little space between them as possible. The rack should be straight and centered on the spot. When your opponent racks for you, periodically check the rack to keep him honest. Some players choose to rack their own. A solid rack will yield a good spread and increase your probability of making balls.

### Racking Properly in 9-Ball

- Rack the 1 through 9 balls on the opposite end of the table you will break from.

- Place the 9 ball in the middle and the 1 ball in the front. The remaining balls can be in any order.

- The 1 ball needs to be centered on the foot spot.

- Rack the balls as tightly as possible. Doing this will make the balls spread apart after the break.

### Loose Rack in 9-Ball

- Sometimes the 1 ball or the back ball may come loose when racking.

- If you see the balls move while your opponent racks, you may want to double-check to make sure they are racked tightly.

- When you have a loose rack, politely ask your opponent to re-rack for you.

- When the balls are loose, some of the cue ball energy is lost when it strikes. The balls will not spread out as well.

Remember to use your best judgment when checking the rack. Not all tables or racks will rack the balls perfectly frozen together. As long as a good effort was made to create a strong rack, you will get a decent break from them. If obvious spaces exist, you should have the balls racked again.

Some racks are specially designed to rack the balls tighter. Many times these racks are used in professional events. These racks may also save time between games by giving players a better rack with fewer attempts.

## *Crooked Rack in 9-Ball*

- At times you may notice that the rack is not lined up properly.

- Because you need to hit the 1 ball full for best results when breaking, you should make sure the rack is straight.

- A good way to check to see if the rack is crooked is by lining up your cue stick across the foot spot between the diamonds on each side.

- Don't hesitate to ask your opponent for a re-rack when you see a crooked rack.

## *Racking off the Spot in 9-Ball*

- A rack of balls should be centered on the foot spot for a good break.

- The balls need to be re-racked when you see a portion of the spot showing.

- When balls are off the spot, it decreases your chances of making a ball on the break.

- It is important that you ask that the balls be re-racked for you.

# BREAKING
## Making balls on the break will give you a chance to decide the first shot

A good break can give you a chance to break and run. The more balls that drop on the break, the fewer balls that need to be cleared off the table.

In 9-Ball you must strike the 1 ball first, and four object balls need to hit a rail, or a ball has to be pocketed. Depending on the league or tournament, fouls on the break differ. You will need to check with your league rule book or tournament director before you start playing. A scratch on a legal break results in ball-in-hand anywhere on the table for the opponent.

You can win the game by making the 9 ball on the break without scratching. If you scratch, the 9 ball gets spotted, and the opponent shoots.

### Breaking in 9-Ball, Position 1

- This is one of the most common places to break from and also yields the best chances of making balls.

- Place the cue ball near the line at the second diamond.

- Line the cue ball straight on with the 1 ball and the second-to-last ball in the rack opposite the side you break from.

- Bridge your hand on the table behind the cue ball.

### Cue Ball Contact Point for Break, Position 1

- Aim for a full hit on the 1 ball from where you break.

- Use a center or just below center ball hit on the cue ball.

- It is ideal to make a ball on the break and also bring the cue ball back to the center of the table.

- This is a good location to make your next shot when you make a ball on the break.

102

As with 8-Ball, break from different positions to find the most probable spot to make balls from. Sometimes you may need to adjust your position depending on how the balls are racked.

The breaking area is from behind the line across the table at the second diamond. Place the cue ball near this line to give it more momentum when striking the rack.

## Breaking in 9-Ball, Position 2

- Another good position to break from is with the cue ball approximately one ball away from either of the side rails.

- Bridge your hand on the side rail for more stability in your stroke.

- Place the cue ball within a comfortable distance near the second diamond.

- Pay more attention to accuracy than the speed of your break stroke.

## Cue Ball Contact Point for Break, Position 2

- Break the rack solid with a full hit on the 1 ball from your breaking spot.

- Use a center or just below center hit on the cue ball.

- You want to maintain control of the cue ball and, ideally, get it back to the center of the table.

- The last thing you want to do is lose control of the cue ball and scratch on a 9-Ball break.

9-BALL

# PATTERNS IN 9-BALL
## You can visualize a pattern when you know which ball to shoot; learn to choose the right one

Pattern play in 9-Ball is more difficult than in 8-Ball because you are playing position for one ball. In 8-Ball, if you get out of position, you may have another ball to shoot at. To become a good 9-Ball player, recognizing patterns is an important part of your game. The more you play, the easier it will be to find the correct patterns.

When playing 9-Ball, look for the patterns that are free of obstacles. When playing position on your next shot, avoid moving other balls around. Every time the cue ball goes into another ball, you run the risk of scratching or losing position. At times you have no choice but to hit into another ball, or you may have to break up a cluster. Many times players will

### Pattern Play

- Here you should shoot the 2 ball into the corner pocket and bring the cue ball up table.

- Play the 3 ball into the top right corner pocket with low left English to get position on the 4 ball.

- Shoot the 4 ball into the top left corner pocket and draw back for position on the 5-9-ball combination.

- Always look for the easiest way to get from one position area to another.

### Breaking Up Clusters

- The 5, 6, and 9 balls are clustered and need to be broken out.

- Shoot the 1 ball into the corner pocket and let the cue ball roll forward toward the rail for an angle at the 2 ball.

- Shoot the 2 ball into the lower left corner pocket, leaving an angle to shoot the 3 ball into the same pocket.

- The cue ball will come off the rail and break open the cluster of balls, allowing the run to continue.

let the cue ball run free into a small cluster of balls and have no position for the next shot. Instead, look at the cluster and check for a pocket that your object ball can go into. Play for the position rather than for the breakout.

When you first learn 9-Ball, you will find that you need to move the cue ball around the table more than in 8-Ball. Because you are playing position on only one ball each shot, at times you have to make the decision on whether to play safe or go for the shot. This decision will depend on your level of play. If you are a strong player and feel that the shot is very makeable, then you would go for it. If you are a newer player to the game and have a safe that you can play, then play the safe. Always play within yourself.

## Play for Position

- It is better to play position for the 3 ball than to attempt to break it out.

- Shoot the 1 ball into the lower left corner pocket and bring the cue ball back to the middle of the table for position on the 2 ball.

- Make the 2 ball and get the proper angle so the cue ball can get position for the 3 ball.

- The 3 ball can then go into the corner pocket and you can continue your run out.

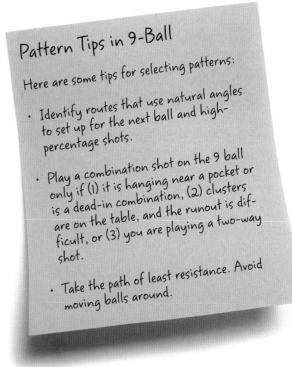

Pattern Tips in 9-Ball

Here are some tips for selecting patterns:

- Identify routes that use natural angles to set up for the next ball and high-percentage shots.

- Play a combination shot on the 9 ball only if (1) it is hanging near a pocket or is a dead-in combination, (2) clusters are on the table, and the runout is difficult, or (3) you are playing a two-way shot.

- Take the path of least resistance. Avoid moving balls around.

# PLAYING SAFE
## Defense wins 9-Ball games; many options make it more favorable for you

At times you may not have a three-ball run when playing 9-Ball. If you have clusters, they can be used to your advantage by playing a safety. As you are deciding when to play safe, look at where the clusters are and how you can get to them. It may make more sense to play safe on the ball before the problem ball instead of taking the risk of breaking it out.

Another way to play safe is by intentionally fouling. You should do this when you are able to lock a ball up and make it more difficult for your opponent to make that ball. Even if your opponent gets ball-in-hand, he will be forced to break it out or play safe back.

If you are in a situation where the 9 ball is hanging near a

**Playing Safe in 9-Ball**

When you play safe, these are some of the questions to ask yourself:

- Can you hide the cue ball from the object ball?

- Can you place sequential object balls at opposite ends of the table?

- Can you leave your opponent a long difficult shot or a bank shot?

- Is the table layout such that you cannot make a good hit, and the 9 ball is hanging near a pocket? You should pocket the 9 ball and give your opponent ball-in-hand. It is better for you if he has to run the table out rather than play an easy combination.

*Playing a Cue Ball Safe*

- The 1 ball is in a difficult position to make into a pocket.

- Play a safe. Trying the combination here is too risky. If you miss, you will leave your opponent wide open for the runout.

- You want to aim full into the 1 and hit the cue ball with a little bit of draw.

- Draw the cue ball to freeze on the 4 ball, leaving your opponent with no shot.

pocket, but you are unable to combo it in early, or you are left hooked behind another ball, you need to think about your best option. One defensive play is to intentionally foul by pocketing the 9. The 9 ball is the only ball that gets re-spotted on the table. Doing this is a useful strategy when the table setup is unfavorable for a runout. Doing this will also prevent your opponent from having the chance to combo it in early.

You can play safe in other ways. You can hit directly into an object ball to get it on the opposite end of the table. Use multiple rails if you need to. You can also hit off the side of an object ball to get your cue ball to hide behind other balls.

## Playing a Carom Ball Safe

- You have two choices here. The first choice is to cut the 1 ball in the corner and go for the runout.

- The second choice is to play safe.

- Hit the left side of the 1 ball and have the cue ball go two rails behind the 8 and 9 balls.

- Doing this will leave your opponent with no shot, and you may get ball-in-hand. Whenever you are unsure of making a shot, look for a good safe.

## Playing a Pocketed Ball Safe

- Here you can try to hit the 1 ball, but there is no guarantee you will get a good hit.

- Notice that you have no easy way to run the table. With ball-in-hand, your opponent can combo the 9.

- Because you can see the 9 ball, you should pocket it now. The 9 ball will get spotted.

- Your opponent will have to work harder to run out the rack.

# TIPS & STRATEGIES

## Strategies depend on whether you are a lower- or higher-skilled player

Many beginning players and lower-skilled players enjoy 9-Ball because they already know which ball to shoot at. Much of the decision making used in 8-Ball is reduced. Instead, decide whether you should play offense or defense. 9-Ball is a good game to improve your shot making, positioning, and kicking ability and to expand your thought process in defensive play.

Many lower-skilled players face difficult shots after pocketing a ball. Having to shoot difficult shots is one way to increase your shot-making ability. Most often you will concentrate on making your shots. If you are not confident in making a ball, consider a safety. Beginning players should focus more on making one ball at a time.

*Offense Strategies for Lower Skill Levels*

- Try to shoot the balls that you are capable of making. If you are unsure of a shot, look for a safe.

- In league play every ball counts, so you want to run as many as you can.

- Pay attention to the cue ball. The more you move it around, the better your chances of scratching.

- Use center ball hits on the cue ball as much as possible. Putting English on the cue ball will make the shot more difficult.

*Defense Strategies for Lower Skill Levels*

1 Ball

- You have two options here.

- Offensively you could go for the 1 ball in the corner and bring the cue ball back across for the 2.

- Defensively shoot directly into the 1 ball just hard enough to get it to the rail and a little farther.

- Your cue ball will land in the middle of the table, and the 1 ball will land near the center of the back rail.

Two-way shots are a good option when you are not sure of a shot and are unable to identify a good safety. In case you miss, you will earn yourself another chance back at the table or ball-in-hand.

Higher-skilled players are more likely to position themselves better to run a table. Again, you want to take higher-percentage shots. If you get out of position, consider locking up balls or hiding them when you have a difficult table to run. Changing the table layout will give you a better opportunity to get back to the table. More-advanced players focus on finding three-ball patterns and getting a good leave for their next shot.

Intentional fouls come in handy when you are unsure you can make a good hit. Pass the table back to your opponent without giving him a shot. Knock an object ball toward the next ball in sequence or another ball to create a cluster and stop a run. Doing this is also a good option when your opponent can't get a breakout.

## *Offense Strategies for Higher Skill Levels*

- When you are good at banking and are faced with this situation, you should go for the shot.

- Shoot into the 1 ball to bank it into the corner pocket.

- Your cue ball will come back toward the center of the table, leaving you with a good shot on the 2 ball.

- You should give yourself a slight angle so you can position the cue ball fairly straight on the 3 ball to roll it up into the corner.

## *Defense Strategies for Higher Skill Levels*

- When you are weaker at banking and faced with this situation, consider playing smart.

- With the same idea as when you choose offense, execute a two-way shot.

- Hit the 1 ball full as though you are banking it. Execute with a stop shot to sit the cue ball behind the 8.

- If you miss the bank, you will increase your chance to get ball-in-hand. You will still have a shot at the 2 if you make it.

9-BALL

# BASIC RULES
## The game of choice before 9-Ball was 14.1 Continuous/Straight Pool

One of the longest-running games in reference to the actual time played in pool is 14.1 Continuous, better known as "Straight Pool." For many years all the world championships played Straight Pool—races to 150 points. The championships in Straight Pool were big news. All the major newspapers covered the championships. Ralph Greenleaf, Willie Mosconi, Irving Crane, Joe Balsis, and Luther Lassiter were just a few of history's great Straight Pool players.

Back in the 1960s ABC's *Wide World of Sports* covered the national Straight Pool championships. They were held in Johnson City, Illinois. All the great players of the day went there to compete. They played not only Straight Pool, but also One Pocket, Bank Pool, and Three-cushion billiards. Those were the days when Straight Pool reached its highest popularity.

Straight Pool tournaments sometimes lasted for weeks.

### Straight Pool Rules

- Each player lags a ball from behind the head string and shoots it up table and back. The player closest to the foot rail has the choice of shooting the opening break or making his opponent shoot it.

- Two balls plus the cue ball must hit a rail on the opening break.

- If you pocket a ball or balls and scratch, those balls are spotted, and you lose a point.

- You can shoot at any ball on the table. On a scratch the cue ball goes behind the head string.

*After the Opening Break in Straight Pool*

- If the breaker plays a good safety on the opening break, you are left with the cue ball on the bottom rail and nothing good to shoot at.

- You should check the rack carefully, looking for some combinations that are dead into a pocket.

- If you have no shot, then you have to look for a good safety to play.

- You want to leave your opponent with a safety or a difficult shot.

Participants played a round-robin format or double elimination with races to 150 points. Willie Mosconi was considered the greatest Straight Pool player ever. He holds the world record with a run of 526 balls. What makes such a run so remarkable is the amount of concentration it takes. You must be able to run the fourteen balls on the table and leave the last ball along with the cue ball in a position that allows you to pocket the ball and break open the rack.

There has been more and more movements to bring the game of Straight Pool back into the limelight. Each year, it seems that a few new Straight Pool tournaments are appearing. Most pool enthusiasts consider Straight Pool as the best test of skill for players to compete in.

## Using a Break Ball

- At the end of each rack, the last ball on the table stays up, and the cue ball remains where it is.

- You want to leave yourself an angle on that last ball where you can pocket it and also have the cue ball go into the rack.

- Doing this is how you keep a run going.

- Try to get an angle that will give a good hit into the rack to spread the balls apart.

### Additional Straight Pool Rules

- Straight Pool games are played to 150 points, although you can shorten them to 100 or even 50.

- Each ball is worth one point. The numbers on the balls do not mean anything.

- For each scratch you lose one point. If you scratch three consecutive times, you lose the three points plus fifteen more as penalty. You are then required to re-rack the balls and shoot the opening break.

- You continue shooting until you miss. Then your opponent shoots. When all the balls are pocketed except one, you rack the balls, leaving the cue ball and the object ball where they are.

# OPENING BREAK

## This is probably one of the few games in which you want your opponent to break

The opening break in Straight Pool is a soft and controlled shot. You do not want to open the rack up and give your opponent the chance for a big run. At the opening break shot and after a three-scratch violation are the only times when you have to drive two balls plus the cue ball to a rail. On all other shots, you are required to drive any ball to the rail only after another ball has been contacted. Straight Pool has no "ball-in-hand anywhere" fouls. All table scratches are played from where the cue ball ends up. All pocket scratches are played with ball-in-hand from behind the head string.

The opening break is a defensive shot. You want to leave your opponent with no shot so that he has to attempt a

*Breaking in Straight Pool*

- On the opening break the breaker must send two balls to a rail along with the cue ball.

- The best option is to place the cue ball just right of center of the head spot.

- Hit the cue ball at about one o'clock. You want to hit the ball at the far right side on the back row of the rack.

- Try to have the cue ball go three or four rails and freeze on the bottom cushion.

*Corner Ball Paths in Straight Pool*

- Ideally you want the two corner balls on the edge of the rack to return to their original position.

- Although doing this is difficult, most times you will still leave your opponent a tough shot.

- Speed and accuracy are important in the opening break.

- Practice getting just the right hit on the end ball to send it to the rail and back into the rack.

safety on you. The strategy is to make the other player shoot at something that may break open some balls and allow you a chance at a big run. If you decide to play Straight Pool, you need to work on your break.

## *Desired Cue Ball Location in Straight Pool*

- After the break you want to send the cue ball three or four rails and try to freeze it to the head rail.

- This position of the cue ball will make it difficult to pocket a ball.

- It will also make it difficult to play a safety from.

- Practice this shot often and get the correct speed. You want to give yourself the best opportunity to return to the table.

## *Successful Break in Straight Pool*

- By making a successful break on the opening shot, you put yourself in the best position possible.

- Your opponent now has to play a difficult safe, go for a tough shot, or take an intentional scratch.

- All three scenarios are favorable to the breaker.

- The better you become at making a good break, the better your chance of winning the game.

# HOW TO SCORE

## In older pool rooms, some tables had scoring beads, whereas other tables had number counters

Each ball in Straight Pool is worth one point. The numbers on the ball have no bearing in this game. As a matter of fact, you could play this game with a cue ball and all of the other balls painted red.

You must call each shot and, when you pocket the ball, you receive one point. If the ball you called goes into the called pocket and another ball also falls in, then you will receive two points and so on. You keep receiving points for each ball pocketed until you miss.

If you pocket a ball and scratch the ball comes up and is spotted. If you cannot place it on the spot, position the ball straight back from the foot spot. You are looking for a clear

*Scoring*

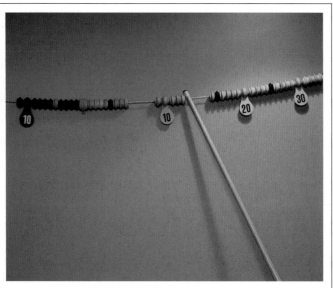

- Beads are one of the most popular ways to keep score for straight pool.

- The beads are strung up on a wall or sometimes above the pool table. Most sets have fifty beads on each side.

- You can also use beads to keep score when playing in a 9-Ball match.

- You can use your cue stick to move the beads, if you like, but it is probably better to use a house cue. You don't want to damage your shooting cue.

*Continuing Play*

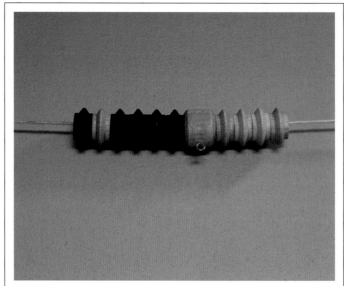

- Each side of the scoring beads usually has fifty beads. The beads have a marker at every fifth bead and every tenth bead.

- This arrangement makes it easier to keep track of the score.

- You can walk into any room where a game is taking place and instantly know the score.

- Beads are also used to keep track of games won during a 9-Ball match.

area to place it. You deduct one point from your score for the scratch. If you miss a ball and scratch, you simply take a point away from your score, and the turn passes to your opponent, making the cue ball-in-hand behind the head spot.

At the end of each rack, the total number of balls made during that rack needs to add up to fourteen. You may wonder how this can happen if a player scratches. When a player scratches, the scratch comes off his total score, not the score for that rack. For example, if the scratch occurs during the opening break, the player who fouled is said to owe two. You would remove two points at the end of the rack.

## Scoring Fouls

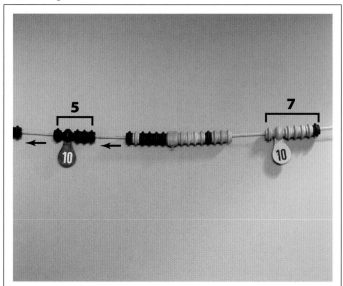

- When a player makes a foul and you are using the bead system, the deducted point must come off the total score.

- Each rack should always add up to fourteen balls.

- If a player scratches, and you deduct the point from the rack total, you will not be able to keep track of how many balls were made that rack.

- When a scratch occurs, slide a point off your total score and then slide a point onto your rack total.

## Continuous Scoring between Racks

- At the end of each rack, the total number of balls should add up to fourteen.

- Using the beads or a counter makes keeping score easy.

- If a player scratches on the opening break, then the total for that rack would be twelve.

- For example, the player who fouled on the opening break lost two points, so fourteen minus two equals twelve.

# SAFETY PLAY

## With the exception of One Pocket, there is more safety play in 14.1 than in any other game

From the opening break, safety play is an important part of winning at 14.1 Continuous/Straight Pool. Good players are capable of runs of fifty, seventy-five, or one hundred balls and more. For the average player, just getting through a single rack would be difficult.

You want to pocket as many balls as possible. When you are left with no shot, you need to play a safe. You try never to leave an open table with the balls spread out for your opponent. Safeties can be anything from leaving the opponent with a long cut shot to freezing him to another ball. Knowing when to play safe and when to go for it is something that only you can decide. The score, strength of opponent, the

*Playing Safe, Scenario 1*

- Because you have no shot here, a safety is the only play.

- Hit full into the 13 ball, which will drive the 15 ball to the rail.

- The cue ball will freeze on the 13 and 11 balls, leaving your opponent with no shot.

- Do not hit this shot too hard. You don't want the 15 ball to come back up the table and leave your opponent with a shot.

*Playing Safe, Scenario 2*

- The defensive strategy here is to get a thin hit on the right side of the 2 ball.

- Doing this will freeze the 2 ball to the rack.

- Send the cue ball up to the far end of the table and try to leave it on or as close as you can to the end rail.

- Doing this will force your opponent into a long safety shot.

table, size of pockets, and confidence are just some of the factors you must weigh before shooting.

Safety is usually the better play if you are having a difficult time deciding what to do. In Straight Pool players can sit for long periods of time and are not warmed up when they come back up to the table. Unlike in 9-Ball, where the game is fast, and you rarely have to wait for more than a couple of minutes, you could have ten to fifteen minutes between shots in Straight Pool.

The best safeties are executed when you can freeze the cue

ball to the rack while freeing up some balls on the opposite side. Doing this forces your opponent into a difficult safe or a scratch. Always look for the safety option. Even if you play a bad safe, it is far better than opening up the rack and giving your opponent an easy run.

## Playing Safe, Scenario 3

- A thin hit on the left side of the 2 ball will send the 2 ball into the rack.

- The cue ball will go two rails and travel down toward the foot rail.

- Doing this will leave your opponent a difficult shot in which he will most likely have to play a safe.

- Clustering balls makes it tough on your opponent to pocket a ball.

## Playing Safe, Scenario 4

- This safety play is one of the easier ones to perform.

- A simple stop shot on the 13 ball will freeze the cue ball to the 4 ball, leaving your opponent with no shot.

- Be careful not to hit this shot too hard and send the 13 ball all the way around the table.

- You want to hit it just hard enough to stop the cue ball on the 4.

117

# THE MOST IMPORTANT SHOT

## Leaving the cue ball and the break ball in the correct position will lead to big runs

At the end of a rack, when you have just two balls (the cue and the object ball) left on the table, you need to position yourself so that you can pocket the object ball and have the cue ball break open the next rack. This will allow you to continue your run. If you are serious about playing this game, you should watch videos of professionals playing Straight

Pool. It is a thing of beauty. They are able to control the cue ball throughout the entire game. When they reach the end of the rack, observe how they play for position on the last ball. The last ball is the most important shot, the shot that will hopefully keep the run going.

Various positions allow you to pocket the last ball and send

*Break Shot, Scenario 1*

- The 1 ball is in perfect position to be pocketed in the corner and have the cue ball break open the rack.

- You must really concentrate on pocketing the 1 ball.

- Do not shoot this shot at break speed. You want to

hit it firmly, but you also need to hit it with control.

- If you hit the rack too hard, the balls will come off the rail and group back together in the middle of the table.

*Break Shot, Scenario 2*

- A thin cut on the 1 ball will pocket the 1 ball in the corner, and the cue ball will come off the rail and hit the rack of balls.

- Concentrate on making the 1 ball.

- Hit this shot with a firm stroke.

- One of the dangers of this break shot is that if you hit it too hard with draw, the cue ball may end up at the foot end of the table.

the cue ball into the rack. Some players like to blast it like a break shot, whereas others hit it with medium speed and break out a few balls at a time. If you blast the rack, you will spread balls all over the table, which could lead to some long shots. If you break it out with medium speed, most of the balls will stay at one end, but here you run the risk of having more balls clustered. Many times the shot will depend on the table, the cloth used, and the type of balls. If the balls are spreading apart easily, then you can use a medium stroke. If the balls are staying clustered, you need to hit the break shot

harder. As you get closer to the end of the rack, you have to pick out your break ball. Sometimes it is already in perfect position, whereas other times you may have to move it a bit.

## Break Shot, Scenario 3

- The 1 ball is in good position for the break.

- Hit this shot with top right English. Use a firm stroke.

- The cue ball will pocket the 1 ball and hit the rack.

- The cue ball will then go three rails and end up at the center of the table. You need to hit this shot with enough speed to get it to go the three rails.

## Break Shot, Scenario 4

- The side-pocket break shot is an effective way to really scatter the balls.

- You want the cue ball to hit the front two balls on the rack so you will not scratch.

- If you hit the side of the rack, the cue ball may go right into the corner pocket.

- Take your time and make the ball in the side pocket.

# WORLD RECORDS

## Willie Mosconi's 526-ball run has stood for more than fifty years

The world record for Straight Pool was set in March 1954 by Willie Mosconi, who ran 526 balls during an exhibition in Springfield, Ohio. This was done on a 4-by-8-foot table. Straight Pool tournaments are typically held on 9-foot tables, but this particular run was done during an exhibition. It is a record that will be difficult to break because only a few Straight Pool tournaments are held nowadays. Most tournaments held today are either in 9-Ball or 10-Ball.

Straight Pool hit its peak during the 1940s, '50s, and '60s. Tournaments were long and physically—as well as mentally—demanding. Players dressed in a suit and tie for their matches. The games played to 150 points, and they were round-robin events.

Videos show many of the great players of yesterday playing Straight Pool (see the Resources for more information).

*Willie Mosconi*

- Willie Mosconi holds the world record for the high run in Straight Pool at 526 balls.

- Willie was inducted into the Billiard Congress of America Hall of Fame in 1968 at the age of fifty-five.

- Willie not only taught Paul Newman how to play pool in the movie *The Hustler* but also appeared in a few scenes.

- Willie Mosconi died on September 12, 1993, of a heart attack.

### Men's Straight Pool World Records

- The high run was 526 balls by Willie Mosconi in 1954.

- Mike Eufemia is said to have run 626 balls, but this run was contested when it was discovered that nobody witnessed the run from beginning to end.

- Thomas Engert had a high run of 492 balls.

- Allen Hopkins had a high run of 421 balls.

- Earl Strickland had a high run of 408 balls.

Willie Mosconi's nickname was "Mr. Pocket Billiards." Willie began practicing his pool skills at a young age by moving small potatoes around with a broomstick. At around seven years old, he began playing challenge matches that his father set up for him. At eleven he was playing exhibitions.

In 1933 Willie played in the World Straight Pool Championship and lost in the finals to Erwin Rudolph. From there Willie went on to win the World Straight Pool Championship a record fifteen times. Willie retired from tournament play in 1966.

## Women Straight Pool Players

- One of the best Straight Pool players among women is Ewa Laurance.

- Ewa was ranked number one female player in the early 1990s.

- Jean Balukas was the most dominant women straight pool player in the 1970's

and 80's. Jean won the U.S. Open championship 7 years in a row.

- Today there are many great women straight pool players including Jasmin Ouschan, who finished third in the 2008 World Championships which was open to both men and women.

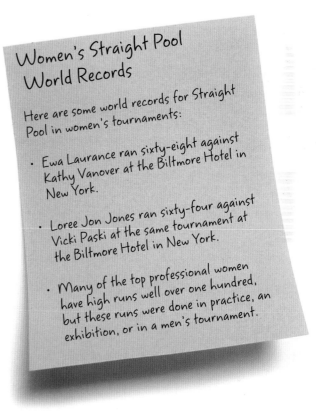

### Women's Straight Pool World Records

Here are some world records for Straight Pool in women's tournaments:

- Ewa Laurance ran sixty-eight against Kathy Vanover at the Biltmore Hotel in New York.

- Loree Jon Jones ran sixty-four against Vicki Paski at the same tournament at the Biltmore Hotel in New York.

- Many of the top professional women have high runs well over one hundred, but these runs were done in practice, an exhibition, or in a men's tournament.

# ONE POCKET BASICS
## Playing this game will help you become a better all-around player

The game of One Pocket is perhaps the most challenging in billiards. The skill set required to play the game is vast, involving shot-making ability, precise cue ball control, and strategy as intense as that in the game of chess.

The object of the game is fairly simple. Pocket balls into your own pocket while preventing your opponent from pocketing balls into his.

The breaker chooses one of the corner pockets at the

foot of the table. Any ball that goes into that pocket will be scored for that player. The second player will automatically be assigned the other corner pocket.

Any ball that goes into your pocket is yours regardless of who played the shot as long as no foul was committed. Any ball that falls into one of the four unassigned pockets is spotted at the foot spot after the player's turn unless no more balls are on the table. If the foot spot is occupied, the ball will

### The Opening Break

### After the Opening Break

- When breaking, you must be careful not to scratch.

- Shoot the right side of the lead ball thin to carom into the second ball.

- Use left English when shooting from the right side or right English when

shooting from the left side of the table.

- Be careful not to scratch on the break because you will owe a ball and most likely leave your opponent a good shot at his pocket.

- This photo shows how a common break shot looks.

- The ideal location of the cue ball is near the cushion at the second diamond as shown.

- In this example you choose the left corner pocket to score in. Notice how after

the break the 5 ball is near your pocket, and also a couple of other balls are on your side.

- The most important result is that your opponent is left without a shot at his pocket.

be spotted along the center line behind the spot as close to the spot as possible.

If the cue ball scratches or jumps off the table, it is considered a foul. Any balls that were pocketed are spotted, and the opponent will receive ball-in-hand behind the head string. If an object ball jumps off the table, it is considered a foul, and the ball is spotted.

All fouls are one penalty ball, which is spotted immediately. If the player has no balls to his credit, then the player owes a ball. Once the player legally pockets a ball, it will be spotted

at the end of his turn. It is easy to remember how many balls are owed by leaving a penny near your pocket.

Because fifteen balls are available, the first to gain eight balls is the winner.

## Controlling the Game

- Controlling the game is important.

- Here you did not pocket the 5, but you hit it with good speed where the 5 remained close to the pocket.

- Because the ball is now a threat, your opponent is forced to play a defensive shot.

- Even though you missed, you likely will score this ball because it is difficult for your opponent to knock it away from your pocket.

## Two-way Shot

- Here is another example of good One Pocket strategy. You missed the 5, but you left it in a great position.

- Even though your opponent has balls near his pocket you left him no shot.

- You also gave yourself a chance to steal the 3 ball and the 2 ball if the 5 ball went.

- You'll always want to leave the cue ball in a position where your opponent cannot remove balls near your pocket.

# ONE POCKET PATTERN PLAY
## Recognizing patterns will strengthen your offensive play

Offense is important in One Pocket when you have the chance to run balls. Running balls in One Pocket is much more difficult than in other games because you can make balls in only one pocket instead of multiple pockets. When the opportunity arises for a run, you should analyze the table for the best way to make balls.

Remember that you should take care when choosing the first ball even in a simple three-ball run. Sometimes having an option to shoot either of two balls can be taken for granted and mess up your run, affording you only one or two balls.

You may have opportunities to make simple runs of two or three balls increase to runs of five or six balls by incorporating a less-difficult bank shot. If you are good at banking, your best option would be to try the five- or six-ball run.

To play better One Pocket you must learn how to manage your game to the way you are playing at the time. Doing this

### Three-ball Run

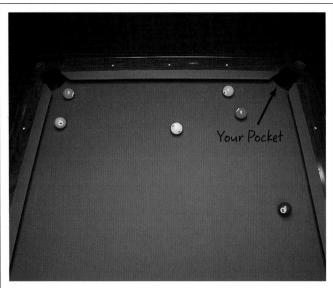

Your Pocket

- Win a game with a simple three-ball run.

- Remember to concentrate so you do not make the run harder than it should be.

- Accomplish this by making the 1 ball and playing position for the 2 ball. Position-

ing for the 3 ball will be easy.

- If you played position for the 3 ball and ended up straight in, you would draw the cue ball toward the side and back across for position on the 2 ball.

### When to Bank

Your Pocket

- You need two balls, and your opponent needs only one ball.

- A good strategy here is to go for the bank shot on the 2 ball.

- Then make the ball that is hanging in your opponent's

pocket and follow it with the cue ball to scratch.

- The last object ball plus one more will be spotted, and your opponent will have a more difficult shot in order to get out.

is what separates a good One Pocket player from a great one. All players have days when they are off in their shot making and cue ball control. These are the days when you should go for more simple patterns, although you are running fewer balls.

Many times you have a couple of patterns from which to choose, such as one in which you would be removing balls from your opponent's side of the table to make balls in your pocket or in which you would be going up table to make balls in your pocket. Sometimes choosing a more difficult pattern is better as long as it would leave your opponent a tougher time making balls in his pocket if you miss.

## Low-risk Bank

- In this situation it is a better choice to take a bank shot than to play position for the 3 ball.

- It is a low-risk shot because you will be removing a ball from your opponent's pocket.

- The 1 ball makes the pocket bigger, increasing your chance of pocketing the ball.

- Your cue ball will end up in a good position to make the 1 ball after you make the bank.

## Using the Rails

- For this situation you need all three balls, and your opponent needs only one.

- This is where your knowledge of banking comes into play because many good One Pocket players know this shot.

- When you bank, the 1 ball, the cue ball will come off the rail and set you up behind the 2 ball for your next shot.

- When you make the 2 ball you will be in a good position to make the 3 ball for the win.

125

# ONE POCKET STRATEGIES
## Here are a few veteran moves and tips to add to your tool kit

The best way to learn the game of One Pocket is to play with a seasoned veteran. This game has so many strategy moves that it would be impossible to learn them on your own. It is truly a game of patience and strategy.

If you are the type of player who loves to fire in balls, then One Pocket is probably not for you. If you love the game of chess, then it is more likely that you will enjoy this game. Sometimes a single game of One Pocket can last hours. The game will help you learn to play defense. No other game requires as many defensive plays as the game of One Pocket.

If you come across a good One Pocket player, you can be sure that he is a strong player at just about every other game. It takes much longer to learn the strategies and moves in this game than probably any other pool game. You are always trying to send balls to your side of the table and never leave your opponent a shot.

### Strategy Tip: Two-way Shot

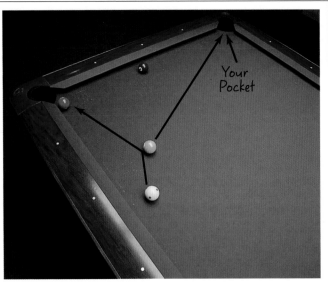

Your Pocket

- This is a situation in which you and your opponent need two balls to win.

- You can pocket the 1 into your corner and get position on the 2.

- If you miss, your opponent will have a shot at the 3 hanging in his pocket.

- It is better to play the 1 and pocket the 3 with the cue ball. Doing this will sacrifice a ball, but you will not give your opponent a shot if you miss.

### Balls in Play

- When you have a lead, consider taking balls out of play.

- In this situation you need two balls, and your opponent needs six.

- If you keep only two balls in play, you have a chance to win the game in one turn.

- Your opponent will have a difficult time making six balls in one turn.

- Balls that are clustered together are already out of play; start sending the rest down table to protect your lead.

Whereas you might take a long shot down the rail in a game of 9-Ball or Straight Pool, you would not take that chance in One Pocket. A miss like that could quickly end the game for you. Most games have times when you take chances. In One Pocket it is far better to play safe than to risk losing the game on a tough shot. As mentioned, you want to learn the game from someone who has been playing it for a long time. Even then, it will take you awhile to learn the correct moves.

## Move Multiple Balls

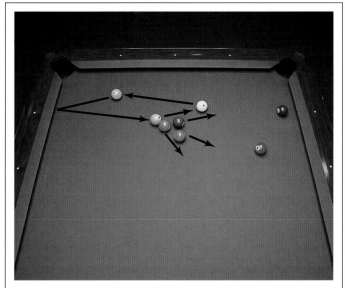

- You have many opportunities when you can move multiple balls to your side of the table in one shot.

- Imagine you need all the balls. If you execute this shot properly, you can prevent your opponent from making a point to win.

- Knock the 1 ball away from your opponent's pocket and send it into the cluster of balls, pushing them toward your pocket.

- The cue ball will remain on your opponent's side of the table, leaving him no easy shot.

## Intentional Scratch

- Here you need two balls, and your opponent needs one ball for the win.

- You want to make the 1 ball in your opponent's pocket and scratch so the object ball gets spotted along with one of your own.

- Your opponent will have cue ball-in-hand behind the line and no open shot.

- It only cost you one ball, but you prevented an imminent loss.

127

# THREE-CUSHION BILLIARDS

## If you want to become a complete player, learn the game of Three-cushion billiards

If you walk into a pool room and see a table that has no pockets, it is a billiard table. When growing up, most of us were used to seeing a pool table that was 7, 8, or 9 feet long with six pockets. A billiard table is 10 feet long and has no pockets.

The game of billiards is more popular in Europe than in the United States. Because there are no pockets, the scoring system is unique. There are three balls, each of which are larger and heavier than what we are used to seeing on a pocket billiard table. The players lag for first shot and also for choice of ball.

The object of the game is to hit your ball into your opponent's ball or the other ball, go three or more rails, and contact the third ball. There are other variations on billiards.

### Rules for Lagging

- Both players go up to the table and lag for the opening shot.

- The balls are placed within the head string and head rail. Both players lag the ball to the far end of the table and back.

- The player whose ball stops closest to the head rail wins the lag.

- The balls may touch the side rail on the lag. If the two balls touch, the player whose ball went across the center line loses the lag.

### Opening Shot

- Each player selects a ball. The winner of the lag gets to take the opening shot or give it up to his opponent.

- The opponent's ball is placed on the head spot.

- The player's ball is placed on a spot to either the left or right of the head spot. The red ball is placed on the foot spot.

- On only the opening shot the red ball must be hit first.

Some players shoot into one of the balls and simply have to hit the other ball in order to score a point. Three-Cushion billiards is considered the hardest because of the minimum of 3 rails needed to be contacted.

To be a great billiard player, you must know the diamond system. Those diamonds on the rail will help you calculate just where to hit your first rail. Some billiard players look at the shot backward and figure out where the ball needs to come off of the last rail. Whatever way you are most comfortable with is the best way to go.

## Scoring Points

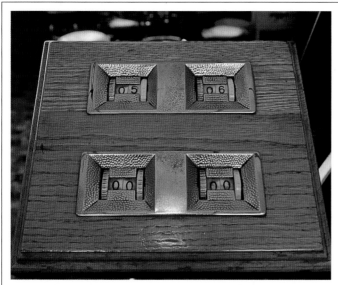

- You must hit your ball first and contact your opponent's ball, go three or more cushions, and hit the red ball.

- You can also hit the red ball first, go three or more cushions, and contact your opponent's ball.

- Also, you can go three or more rails with your ball and hit both the red and your opponent's ball.

- You need to hit three cushions or more in each shot and make contact with both balls to score a point.

### Three-cushion Rules

- There are three balls: red, yellow, and white.

- Players must choose either the yellow or white ball as their cue ball. The players then lag for the opening shot.

- All shots require a minimum of three cushions in order to score a point.

- You must always hit your cue ball first.

- Most games are played to fifteen points.

# THREE-CUSHION EQUIPMENT

## Three-cushion billiards is played on a 10-by-5-foot table with no pockets

Billiards uses different equipment than we are use to seeing in most pool rooms. First, the game uses three colored balls: yellow, white, and red. The balls are larger than those used in 8-Ball or 9-Ball. A billiard ball is 2⁷⁄₁₆ inches in diameter. It is also heavier at about 7.5 ounces.

The table is 10 feet long and 5 feet wide. It is covered with

a green cloth that is designed to play fast. A Pocket billiard table can be converted into a billiard table by placing inserts into each of the pockets. These inserts are available to purchase. This is an inexpensive way to try out the game of Three-cushion billiards on your own table.

The cues used in billiards are usually a bit shorter than the

### Long Bridge

- Because of the length of a billiard table, 10 by 5 feet, a bridge is used quite often.

- You will notice that the bridge is usually a bit longer than what you would find on a Pocket billiard table.

- You want to have your shooting arm parallel to the table. Doing this will allow for a straight follow-through.

- You want to place your other hand on top of the handle so that the bridge doesn't move.

### Billiard Balls

- Modern billiard balls are made from phenolic resin or resilient plastics.

- Billiard balls are 2⁷⁄₁₆ inches in diameter and weigh about 7.5 ounces.

- They are significantly larger and heavier than their Pocket billiards counterparts.

- The three standard balls in most carom billiard games are a completely white cue ball, a second cue ball that is yellow, and a third ball that is red.

cues used in pool. The cue is 54 to 56 inches long and weighs about 18 ounces. The tip is 11 to 12 millimeters in diameter. This diameter allows for a stiffer cue to move the larger and heavier billiard balls around. You can play the game with a regular playing cue that is used in pool. It will not damage your stick.

You will not find many billiard tables in the United States. The game is much more popular in Europe. When you do come across a room that has billiards, generally it has only one or two tables. The games of 8-Ball and 9-Ball have traditionally been the more popular choice here in the United States. Room owners realize that billiard tables take up more space and also will not rent out as frequently as pool tables.

*Billiard Table*

*No Pockets on a Billiard Table*

- The billiard table is 5 feet wide and 10 feet long. This is the size used for world championships.

- The billiard table has a heating system that keeps the slate warm. It is usually kept about 5 degrees warmer than room temperature.

- Heating the slate keeps the moisture out of the cloth.

- Doing this allows the balls to roll faster and the rails to play more consistently.

- Unlike on a Pocket billiards table, a billiard table has no pockets.

- All shots are carom shots that require three or more rails to be contacted.

- The game of billiards is thought to have been founded in the 1800s in France.

- Billiards is not found in many U.S. pool rooms. It was popular in the United States during the early to mid 1900's.

# THREE-CUSHION OPENING SHOT
## To start the game of billiards, you must lag for the opening break

The game of Three-cushion billiards requires a tremendous amount of practice and dedication. Averaging just one point per turn is difficult and is considered professional level. The lag and the opening shot are important. Because the first shot is somewhat easy for top players, winning the lag could get a player out to an early lead. Top players are very good offensively as well as defensively. You would not think there would be much defense in the game, but there is. To really learn this game, you need to find a good player. You will be amazed at some of the shots you can play.

Most of the top players come from Europe, Asia, and Latin America. The most dominant player in the history of Three-cushion billiards is Raymond Ceulemans of Belgium. In 1961 at the age of twenty-three Ceulemans won his first Belgian Three-cushion title. In 1962 he won the Confédération Européenne de Billard Three-cushion Championship.

### Starting the Game

- To begin the game of billiards, both players lag from the foot end of the table.

- The player who lags his ball closest to the foot rail wins the lag.

- The winner has the choice of shooting the opening shot or passing it to his opponent.

- Because the opening shot is considered an easy shot, the winner of the lag usually goes first.

### Sportsmanship in Three-Cushion

- Billiards is considered a gentleman's game and adheres to a strict set of rules.

- Players from all over the world compete in major tournaments.

- As with all major sports, amateur or professional, good sportsmanship is always expected and required.

- Win or lose, be sure to shake hands with your opponent before and after your match.

In 1963 Ceulemans won his first world title at the Union Mondiale de Billard World Three-cushion Championship. He averaged 1.159 and 1.307 points per inning. After winning the title eleven times in a row, his winning streak ended in 1974 when he was defeated by Nobuaki Kobayashi in the finals. Ceulemans won the European Three-cushion championship twenty-three times and was inducted into the Billiard Congress of America Hall of Fame in 2001.

········· GREEN ● LIGHT ·············

If there is a billiard table near you, take the opportunity to play a game. It really is enjoyable. You will be amazed at the speed of the table. You will also learn about bank and kick shots.

## Choosing the Cue Ball

- At the beginning of the game, each player selects a ball. A white cue ball and a yellow cue ball are used.

- The ball that each player chooses will be his throughout the game.

- You can never hit your opponent's ball first. Doing this would result in a foul and loss of shot.

- You can shoot your ball into your opponent's ball or the red ball.

## Game Strategy

- Balls that are close to any of the four corners of the table are easiest to score a point on.

- It is always easier to find the correct angle when a ball is sitting near one of the corners.

- When a ball is in a corner, it becomes a larger target to hit because the cue ball can hit it on the way in or on the way back out.

133

# SPEED POOL
## This game will give you a good workout

Watching Speed Pool is like watching two professional boxers fighting it out in a phone booth. It is crazy! The object of the game is to pocket as many balls as you can in the shortest amount of time. Players run around the table as fast as they can to pocket balls. You need a great deal of stamina and a good eye to play this game.

ESPN has televised Speed Pool events for the past few years. The game does not have many rules. In general you must let the cue ball come to a complete stop before shooting. The object balls can be moving but not the cue ball. In 8-Ball you must call the pocket for the 8 ball.

In 8-Ball the player must shoot in all of the solids, then all of the stripes, and then the 8 ball. In a variation of the game you can shoot at any ball in any order. Players play against the clock, which determines who wins the game. The player who has the best time after three rounds wins. Bring your

### Timing a Speed Pool Game

- Speed is everything in this game. You must be able to move around quickly.

- The really good Speed Pool players are able to stroke the cue one time and shoot.

- You won't have the luxury of looking around at the entire table as you would in a normal game.

- You must be accurate but also think fast.

### Playing Speed Pool

- Wear loose clothes and a good pair of sneakers because you will run around the table at a good pace.

- Using a stop shot is the best way to save time. The less distance the cue ball rolls, the more time you will save.

- Sometimes you may want to miss on purpose to break open a cluster.

- You want to control the cue ball at all times in order to keep your time low.

sneakers, towel, and a big bottle of water for this game. The next *Biggest Loser* TV show might want to consider using this game to aid with weight loss!

· · · · · · · · · · · RED ● LIGHT · · · · · · · · · · · ·

You may want to consult your doctor before playing this game. Make sure to move everything out of the way around the table. You don't want to run into anything when you're playing. Always challenge your less-fit friends. It will be an easy victory for you! Wear a good pair of sneakers so that you won't slide all over the place and be careful not to overdo it.

## Fouls in Speed Pool

- Any pocket and table scratches will add ten seconds to your time.

- Table scratches occur when a player fails to drive a ball to a cushion after a legal hit.

- The cue ball must be still when shooting. All other balls can be moving. It is a ten second foul to hit a moving cue ball.

- Some of the rules vary on the last ball: You may or may not have to call the ball and pocket.

### Speed Pool Rules

- The two most popular games for Speed Pool are 8-Ball and Straight Pool.

- In Speed Pool 8-Ball, you must pocket one of the categories of balls first before moving on to the other category. You then must call your pocket for the 8 ball.

- In Speed Pool Straight Pool, you can shoot any ball on the table.

- You are playing against the clock.

- You will be penalized ten-second fouls on all scratches.

# PILL POOL

## You will need a bottle with numbered beads inside to play this game

Pill Pool, also known as "Kelly pool" or "pea pool," is fun to play when you are in a group of people. This game works best when you have three to six players but can be played with up to fifteen. Each person selects a bead numbered from one to fifteen out of the pill bottle and keeps it a secret from the other players.

The number on the bead corresponds with the numbered ball a player needs to pocket in order to win. When an opponent pockets your ball, you need to disclose that before his next shot, or else you are knocked out of the game.

Rack all fifteen balls with the 1 ball in front, the 2 in the rear right corner, and the 3 ball in the rear left corner. The rest of

### Getting Started in Pill Pool

- Purchase a pill bottle at a local supply store that has numbered beads inside. Normally this is a narrow-necked plastic bottle.

- Shake up the bottle and have each player draw a number to determine the shooting order.

- The person who has the lowest number breaks, and the highest number racks.

- Put the beads back into the bottle, shake it up, and pass it around again to determine the ball needed to win. Remember not to tell anyone what your number is.

### Fouling in Pill Pool

- When a ball is illegally pocketed, it gets spotted.

- The incoming player has an option to take the shot as it lies or pass it back to the player who fouled.

- When the cue ball scratches or lands on the floor, the incoming player has ball-in-

hand behind the line with the same option to take or pass off the shot.

- If the object ball is behind the line when a player has ball-in-hand, it gets spotted.

the balls can be placed in any order. For a legal break, four object balls need to hit a rail.

As in 9-Ball, shoot the balls in numerical order until you pocket your secret ball or knock an opponent out. A foul occurs when you do not hit the lowest-numbered ball first, when any ball does not hit a rail after contacting the lowest-numbered ball, or when the cue ball scratches or ends up on the floor.

Watch how other players approach their shots and see if they try for caroms or combinations to pocket their object ball for the win. You can figure out which ball they are trying to make. Play smart to keep them from pocketing their ball.

The rules have several variations, so come to an agreement on the rules you use before you begin the game. For example, a scoring option (see below) can be used to gain points for pocketing secret balls rather than simply pocketing your secret ball to win.

## How to Win in Pill Pool

- Whenever a player pockets his own secret ball number, he wins the game.

- A player may also win using the scoring option by earning the most points for the rack.

- If your secret ball gets knocked in, you can still earn points. A game ends and points stop accumulating when a player knocks in his own secret ball.

- If no player knocks in his own ball, another rack is played until someone does.

### Pill Pool Scoring Options

- Pocket your winning ball for two points.

- Earn one point for each opponent's ball you pocket.

- An opponent gets one point subtracted as long as he discloses his ball was pocketed before the next shot is taken. If not, the shooter gets two points for the ball of each forfeited opponent.

- If no player pockets his own numbered ball, the game ends after the last player's ball number is pocketed. Play again with double points.

# BANK POOL

## This variation is just as it sounds: You must bank in every shot

Each January a major Bank Pool tournament is held. It is part of an eight-day event at the Derby City Classic in Louisville, Kentucky. Players from all over the world compete in Bank Pool, 9-Ball, and One Pocket. Each event crowns an individual champion and an all-around champion each year. In 2010 Efren Reyes of the Philippines won the all-around championship for these three tournaments. Efren Reyes is widely considered the greatest all-around pool player ever.

If you attend the Derby City Classic, you are in for a great time. Here you can see the best players in the world competing. As with the other games of pool, you may learn more about the game from watching the professionals and those with years of experience than you will from playing.

Bank Pool is a demanding game. Players are required to bank in every shot. Kick shots are not allowed. The player must strike an object ball and send it into one or more rails

### Bank Pool Rules

- Bank five balls in any order (eight balls if using a full rack). The player who pockets the majority of the balls wins.

- The balls are racked the same way as in 9-Ball or 8-Ball, depending on if you play with a full rack.

- All bank shots must start with the cue ball hitting the object ball. No kick shots are allowed.

- All shots must be called.

*Breaking in Bank Pool*

- Players can flip a coin or lag for the break.

- On the break the cue ball may contact any ball first. After contact two object balls must contact a cushion.

- If you are using nine balls, the head ball must be struck first, and at least one ball must pass the side pocket.

- If the breaker pockets a ball, it is put off to the side, and the breaker continues to shoot. When he misses, the ball is then spotted on the foot spot.

and make it in a called pocket. The ball must go into the pocket on the path indicated by the shooter.

To become a great Bank Pool player, you need a great deal of time and practice. So many factors affect a bank shot, and knowing how to compensate for them is critical. Speed, humidity, rubber on the cushions, cloth, and many other variables come into play in Bank Pool. That is why a tremendous amount of skill is needed to become proficient at this game. It also takes a great deal of patience because the game can be frustrating when you start out.

## *Banking Skills*

- Bank Pool is a difficult game to have a run of more than a couple of balls at a time.

- Defense is important for the higher-caliber players.

- Learning Bank Pool will help you with every other game of pool that you play. Being good at banks is a skill that can be used in every game.

- The table conditions play a major factor in this game, so be sure you adjust accordingly. Weather also is an important factor.

## *Use Nine or Fifteen Balls*

- You can start with nine balls instead of fifteen.

- The matches will last longer than regular games of 8-Ball and 9-Ball. This goes for the better players as well.

- Bank Pool will give you more confidence in banking when playing other games.

- It is important to focus on banking practice drills when studying up for a Bank Pool game.

# 10-BALL
## This variation is similar to 9-Ball except for a few rules that make it more difficult

The game of 10-Ball is something new to tournament play but is similar to the game of 9-Ball. However, a few differences make the game of 10-Ball a difficult game to play: The balls are racked similar to 8-Ball, which makes it more difficult to pocket a ball on the break. Also, you must call your shots; pocketing the 10 ball on the break is not a win.

Racking in 10-Ball is similar to in 8-Ball, except you don't have the bottom row of balls. The 10 ball is placed where the 8 ball would be. As in 9-Ball, the 1 ball needs to be the head ball and must be struck first on the break. Try to get a full hit on the 1 ball to help avoid the scratch in the side pocket.

The game of 10-Ball was created to make it more difficult

### 10-Ball Rules

• Making the 10 ball on the break does not win the game. Instead, the ball is spotted, and the player continues to shoot.

• You must call your pocket on every shot.

• You must always hit the lowest-numbered ball on the table first.

• Pocketing the 10 ball must be a called shot by a legal carom, a combination, or a shot as the last ball.

*Racking in 10-Ball*

• You rack the balls the same way as you would in 8-Ball, except you need to remove the bottom row of five balls.

• Place the 10 ball in the middle of the rack. For 8-Ball players, this is equivalent to saying the 10 ball goes where the 8 ball would be.

• Place the 1 ball at the head of the rack.

• Make sure all the balls are touching and racked tightly.

for players to break and run out. It may not seem like much, but that one extra ball adds an extra degree of difficulty. It is one more ball that can end up in a cluster or on a rail. It is also another ball that you have to maneuver around when trying to run out. If you anticipate playing in a 9-Ball tournament, it may not be a bad idea to practice the game of 10-Ball. Although it will be a bit more difficult than 9-Ball, it should help you with your position play. Sometimes, when you use one game to help with another, you can learn new things and at the same time make yourself a better player.

## Breaking in 10-Ball

- You must hit the 1 ball first when breaking.

- You want to hit the 1 ball as full as possible to give you the best chance of pocketing a ball on the break.

- A full hit will also decrease your chances of scratching on the break.

- Ideally you want the cue ball to come back about 2 feet and stay in the middle of the table. This position will give you your best chance at having a shot.

## How to Win in 10-Ball

- The object of 10-Ball is to run the balls in numerical order and pocket the 10 ball for the win.

- You must always hit the lowest-numbered ball on the table first.

- Any other balls that go in while legally pocketing a ball stay in, and you continue to shoot.

- You can make the 10 ball early by calling it in a pocket during a combination or carom shot for the win.

# 7-BALL

## This is the perfect variation for the player without a lot of time

7-Ball is a fast game that does not allow for many mistakes. It is an offensive game that requires players to run out the table. With only one defensive shot allowed per rack, players must play great position and run out all the way to the 7 ball. The 7 ball must be a called shot. This game has many strategies that need to be learned in order to perfect it.

7-Ball was made popular by televised events that were held in Las Vegas during the last 10 years. Top professional players were invited to compete for the championship title and money. The games were fast and full of action, especially with lots of runouts.

7-Ball is a great game to use for practice. It helps you develop better concentration for controlling the cue ball. With the penalty for a miss being ball-in-hand for your opponent, you will find out quickly that your table position and accuracy must be good.

### Racking in 7-Ball

- Racking for 7-Ball is different from racking in any other game. The balls form a circle, as seen in the picture.

- The 1 ball is in the front and on the foot spot. The 7 ball is placed in the center of the rack.

- You want to make sure that all the balls are frozen together. This arrangement will assure a good break.

### Breaking in 7-Ball

- You must hit the 1 ball first when breaking. As in 8-Ball and 9-Ball, you want to get a solid hit on the break.

- If you are not making a ball on the break, move the cue ball to another position.

- If you are still not making a ball on the break, try hitting it at about 90 percent of your normal break speed.

- Hitting the break shot easier may scatter the balls differently.

142

7-Ball is also used by professionals when giving an exhibition. The professionals play challenge matches against members of the audience. Many times the challengers pay money to play against the pros, and often the money is donated to a charity.

Not many 7-Ball tournaments are held at this time. 9-Ball and 8-Ball are still the most popular games. Although 7-Ball may catch on in popularity someday, it is played mostly as a good way to practice.

## How to Win in 7-Ball

- You can win by making all the balls in rotation and putting the 7 ball into a called pocket.

- The 7 ball can be pocketed at anytime during the game as long as it is called.

- Making the 7 ball on the break wins the game.

- If you make the 7 ball on the break and scratch, the 7 gets spotted, and your opponent has ball-in-hand.

### 7-Ball Rules

- The 1 ball must be hit first on the break, and four balls must hit a rail.

- Each player is allowed one called safety. If you do not call safe and you miss any shot, the opposing player gets ball-in-hand anywhere on the table.

- Hit the lowest-numbered ball first, and anything extra that goes in is good, with the exception of the 7 ball.

- You must always call the pocket when attempting to make the 7 ball.

# BOWLIARDS

## You can play this variation alone or with your buddies

The game of Bowliards became popular in the 1980s. The game is a combination of bowling and billiards, hence the name "Bowliards." It is an enjoyable game that will keep you playing for hours.

The game is played with ten balls plus the cue ball. You rack ten balls, with the five balls on the back row left out. A player breaks the balls from behind the head string. Anything that is pocketed stays in.

The scoring mimics the style of ten pin bowling. Each ball is worth one point, with a one-point deduction for a scratch. At the start of each round the player is given a free break. The player then takes his next turn with the cue ball behind the head string. The player plays until a scratch or miss occurs. At this point the player gets the cue ball behind the line and plays again until he scratches or misses; this score represents the second turn. The balls are then counted for the total of

### Playing Bowliards

- Rack up ten balls as shown in the photo and break them.

- Put the cue ball behind the line and shoot at any ball. Keep shooting until you miss or scratch.

- Place the cue ball behind the line again and continue shooting until you miss or scratch.

- If you run out all the balls on your first attempt, it is a strike, your second attempt, a spare, and if you miss twice, you get one point for each ball pocketed.

### Scoring in Bowliards

- Keeping score is similar to keeping score in ten-pin bowling.

- You need to make copies of a bowling sheet. If the player runs out all the balls on his first attempt, you mark it down as a strike by making an "X" in the box.

- If he makes all the balls on the second attempt, you make a slanted line for a spare.

- If he misses both times, you put down the number of balls pocketed. Ten frames complete the game.

that round. Then the balls are re-racked, and the other player takes his turn. If a player clears all the balls on his first turn, it's a strike. If he clears them off on the second attempt, it is a spare. If he misses twice, the player will get one point for each pocketed ball.

Each player will have ten turns at the table. The player with the highest score wins. The great part about this game is that you can play alone. Keep trying to get a higher score each time you play. You can even create a handicap system of your own just like what is done in bowling.

## How to Win in Bowliards

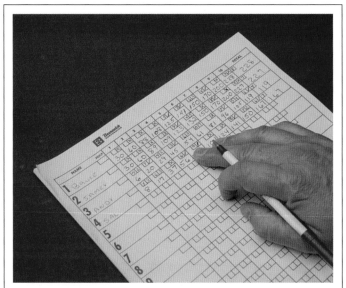

- You can have different rules for the game, depending on how much time you have.

- You can play someone in a game of Bowliards, which means that whoever has the highest score after ten frames wins.

- You can also play three games and add up your scores to see who has the highest total.

- Also, try having a round-robin tournament in which you play everybody in the tournament one time. Whoever has the most victories is declared the champion.

### Bowliards Rules

- Put the cue ball behind the line and shoot at any ball. Shoot until you miss or scratch. If you run out, you get a strike.

- If you miss, you receive the cue ball behind the line and shoot at any ball. If you run out, you get a spare.

- If you miss twice, you get one point for every ball you pocketed. A one-point penalty is assessed for a scratch except on the break.

# LEARNING TRICK SHOTS

## You can easily learn some simple trick shots to amaze your friends

There is no better feeling than making a trick shot in front of all your friends and watching the looks on their faces. Or how about being at a family gathering as your relatives stand around the table to watch you make shots that they have seen only on television?

Trick shots always put a smile on everyone's face. Even your grumpy old uncle will smile when he watches what you can do. The shots in this chapter are great for beginners. They are

easy to set up and can be learned quickly. They don't require a great stroke and can be made using a regular cue.

The key is to practice these shots until you can make them on a consistent basis. Don't get discouraged if some of the shots won't go in for you. Remember that every player has certain shots that he is better at than others. Find the ones that you like best and practice them. After you are confident enough to execute these shots, it will be

### Easy 2 X 2

- Place the 3 ball one ball up from the head spot. Freeze the 4 ball to the 3 ball. Aim it at the right center of the corner pocket.

- Place the cue ball in the center of the table and a half-diamond back from the side pocket.

- Freeze two object balls to the cue ball and aim them at the inside edge of the side pocket.

- Hit with a level cue and firm stroke. Use center or just a touch of high.

### Hit the 1 Ball First

- You will have your buddies guessing on this shot.

- Freeze two balls together on the short rail. You need to gently tap the top of the balls so they stay in place.

- Balance the 1 ball on top of the two balls.

- Place the cue ball at the other end of the table.

- Shoot the cue ball toward the three balls and hit the table with your hand. The vibration will cause the balls to fall, *and you will contact the 1 ball first*.

time to move on to the next group.

The better your stroke is, the better your chance of making a trick shot. For the most part, these twenty-four shots require mostly center ball hits. You need to have a good cue with a good tip on it. A good tip is one that has a half-moon shape. Because you strike mostly center ball, you have less chance of a miscue.

Place the balls as indicated in the photo and the text. Some of the shots will require a slight adjustment, depending on the table and the quality of the balls. Adjustments are minimal with these shots. Practice them as often as you can, and soon they will be automatic.

## Coin Wrapper Shot with Three Balls

- You need two quarter coin wrappers. Cut one wrapper to the height of 1⅜ inches. The other wrapper is normal height.

- Stack the 2 and 3 balls on the wrappers as shown. The wrappers are in the center of the table between the side pockets.

- Place the 1 ball close to the side pocket.

- Place the cue ball in a straight line with the 1, 2, and 3 balls. Simply aim the cue ball at the 1 ball and shoot.

## Which Goes First?

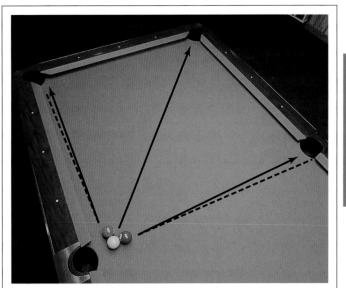

- Place the cue ball one ball out from the middle of a side pocket.

- Freeze the 2 ball to the cue ball and aim it at the right edge of the side pocket.

- Freeze the 3 ball to the cue ball and aim it at the left edge of the corner pocket.

- With a firm, level stroke, shoot the cue ball into the opposite corner pocket, and all three balls will go in.

147

# MORE EASY TRICK SHOTS

## These shots are easy to set up and shoot, but remember to practice

If you are interested in learning trick shots and entering a competition, these shots are the grassroots. Trick shots follow the same philosophies as magic: Beginner magicians first need to learn the basic moves before putting them together in more advanced ways. Some easy card tricks concentrate on one basic move, and the same philosophy applies to trick shots. Start off with a few easy shots, each one highlighting a certain skill or concept. More-advanced shots sometimes

use these skills, but you need to understand how they work before moving on. The key to becoming a good trick shot player is to be able to look at one of these easy shots and know exactly how it works.

No two players learn at the same pace. You may find that you learn faster or slower than your friends, but patience and practice are the keys. Some of the top magicians in the world struggled at the beginning and possibly even thought of

### The Rack Makes Five

- This is a simple way to make five balls at one time.

- Take five balls and, starting at the middle of the side pocket, freeze them together and place a rack up against it.

- Aim the cue ball at the center of the rack.

- Hit with a firm stroke and watch as all the balls go into the side pocket.

### Ball in the Rack

- This is the shot that Tom Rossman used to win his first ESPN *Trick Shot Magic* event.

- Place the rack near the side pocket as shown in the photo.

- Place the 8 ball against the back of the rack. Place the cue ball about 1 foot away.

- With a firm stroke hit the center of the rack. The rack will move forward, and the 8 ball will fall into the pocket.

giving up before getting over that first hump.

None of these basic trick shots damages the cloth, so you can do them at your local pool room. Make sure you always ask permission first. The other benefit is that, although they are basic trick shots, they are entertaining, and practicing them at a pool room will be sure to gather a crowd of all ages. You may find that while you are practicing a shot, a spectator will approach you and ask you to "do it again" or offer a variation that he may have seen on TV or at an exhibition. Give these shots a try and always have fun.

## Mystery Shot

- Place the 2 ball on the foot spot. Freeze the 1 ball to the 2 ball and aim them at the right center of the right corner pocket.

- Put the cue ball in the center of the table in line with the 1 ball. Place the chalk on the rail in line with the cue and the 1 ball. Put a napkin on top of the two balls.

- Aim at the chalk with a medium-speed, level stroke. The balls will come out and pocket in each corner.

## A Little Dab Will Do Ya

- Freeze the 1, 2, and 9 balls on the long rail as shown in the photo.

- Place the cue ball as shown. Shoot directly into the 1. The 9 will travel up the rail and miss to the left of the pocket.

- To make this shot, set it up exactly the same way. But this time with your finger wet the contact point between the 2 and 9 balls.

- Hit it the same way as before, and the 9 ball will go in.

# "WHAT HAPPENED?" SHOTS
## These will keep your audience guessing what will happen

Even though these next four shots are in the beginner chapter, they require a little more skill and practice than the others listed here. Two of these shots require something called a "push stroke." This is not a legal stroke in a normal game of pool, but in trick shots, anything goes. A push shot is just as it sounds. Instead of stroking through the cue ball, you stroke up to the cue ball and stop at the point of contact. With the tip lightly touching the cue ball, you then push through to

make the shot. Although the push shot may take some extra practice to get the hang of, it will open up a lot of shots to add to your collection.

There is a funny story about *Trick Shot Magic* competitor, Andy "The Magic Man" Segal, while he was shooting the "Everything but the Eight" shot. Back in 2004, Andy Segal appeared on ESPN for his second time and brought this shot, slightly modified, into the competition. He altered the setup

### *Simple Squeeze Shot*

- This is an easy trick shot to execute.

- Place the cue ball against the 1 ball as shown. Make sure the balls are frozen together.

- Place the tip of your cue at three o'clock on the cue ball. Make sure the tip touches the cue ball.

- Push the stick forward, and the tip will come off the cue ball on the right-hand side, and the 1 ball will go into the corner pocket.

### *Everything but the Eight*

- Place four balls plus the cue ball on the short rail and freeze them together.

- Place the tip of your cue at nine o'clock on the cue ball.

- With your tip touching the cue ball, simply push your

cue stick forward. Keep the tip on the cue ball for as long as possible.

- All the balls will go into the corner pocket except for the 8 ball.

in a new way that no one had done before by adding a slight gap between one of the balls and the cushion. This caused the balls to react differently than expected, which resulted in his opponent missing the shot. This is just one example of how you can modify these basic concepts to create trick shots that are all your own.

If you let your imagination loose, you will find that these basic skills allow you to create shots that you can post on the Internet to amaze even some of the pros. Don't be surprised if some of the new shots make it to TV trick shot events.

## Kiss Back for the Win

- This is a handy shot to know.

- The 2 ball is against the rail as shown. The 9 ball is hanging in the corner pocket.

- The cue ball is about 1 foot away from the 2 ball. Have all three balls in a straight line.

- Aim the cue ball at the center of the 2 ball. Hit the cue ball just below center. It will kiss back off the 2 and pocket the 9.

## Divide and Pocket

- The 1 and 2 balls are frozen together at a 90-degree angle as shown.

- The 3 and 1 balls have a spacing of 1½ ball. The 3 and 4 are frozen as shown at a 45-degree angle.

- The object of this shot is to shoot into the right side of the 1 ball and carom into the 3, which will separate the 3 and 4.

- The 2 ball will then go cross side.

# HAVING FUN

## Making trick shots will make you and everyone around you feel good

The more you practice, the better you get. And as you get better, you become more confident in your ability to perform these trick shots. You will soon learn about the necessary adjustments needed when a shot doesn't go. You will develop a nice routine so that when you are asked to put on a show or just do a few shots, you will be prepared.

The shots in this chapter work on any size table. It does not matter if it is a 7-, 8-, or 9-foot table, although some of the shots that come up later work better on a 9-foot table.

Trick shots started many years ago. So many of the shots you see here have been around for a while. They may have been altered slightly, but the concept is the same. Many of

### Ride the Cue

- Place the 2 ball on the spot. Freeze the 1 to the 2 as shown. Place the 3 in the corner pocket as shown.

- Place the cue ball just left of center, near the middle of the table.

- Hit the cue ball at eleven o'clock. Aim for a half ball hit on the right side of the 1 ball.

- The cue ball will make the 1 and 2 balls and then travel three rails and hit the cue stick to pocket the 3 ball.

### The Big Y

- The 1 ball is the fourth ball out and centered from the side pocket.

- Freeze the 2 ball to the 1 and aim it at the left edge of the corner pocket. Freeze the 3 ball to the 1 and aim it to the right edge of the corner pocket.

- Put the cue ball near the center of the table and in line with the 1 ball and the side pocket.

- Shoot the cue ball into the 1 ball, and all three balls will go into a pocket.

the shots started as a result of something that happened in a game. You are challenged by what looks like an impossible situation during a regular game, and so you try to figure out how to escape.

Practicing these shots so that you are proficient at them can be addicting. It is sometimes a challenge to figure out just how a shot is made. When you are able to do that, you will become a better trick shot artist.

The key is to have fun. Keeping a smile on your face as you do your shots makes the entertainment that much more enjoyable. After all, how can you not have fun with these shots? They come with a guarantee that you and your audience will smile.

## Sneaky 8 Ball

- The 4 and 8 are frozen together with the tangent line aimed to the left edge of the side pocket.

- The 5 ball is placed at a 45-degree angle toward the long rail.

- Place the cue ball about 1 foot from the 8 ball as shown.

- Shoot the cue ball directly into the 8 ball, and it will go into the side pocket. Hit with medium speed.

## Along the Bridge

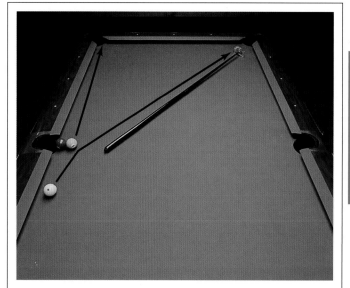

- The cue ball is one chalk from the cushion at the first diamond as shown.

- The 2 is hanging in the center of side pocket with the 1 frozen to it and aimed directly to the center of the opposite side pocket.

- The bridge is placed as shown. The 3 ball is frozen to the bridge head.

- Hit the cue ball a little above center and aim for a half ball hit on the right side of the 1 ball. Hit at medium speed, and all three balls will pocket.

# ADDING PROPS
## With some imagination there is nothing you can't do

Props have been a large part of trick shots for a while now, ever since a book of matches was used to elevate the cue ball from one table to another. Since those days props have become increasingly more complex. As seen in televised events, such as *Trick Shot Magic* or the *World Cup of Trick Shots,* artists use all kinds of props. One famous prop shot is Mike Massey's "Boot Shot," which will be shown later in the book.

A prop is something other than the balls on the table that is used to help with a trick shot. It can be a bridge, rack, chalk, or just about anything else (even a boot). Audiences love props. They always ask how the players came up with that. Most of the prop shots are regular trick shots with a prop added.

The prop serves different purposes. It can help make a shot, or it can be an obstacle to make the shot more difficult. Most any item will do. Someone once said, "Give me any item, and

### Golf Ball Shot

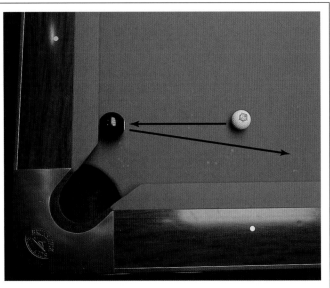

- This is another simple shot that will impress your friends.

- Freeze the 8 ball to the rail near the corner pocket. Place a golf ball about 1 foot away, straight out from the 8.

- Aim the golf ball into the 8 ball, and the 8 will bank cross corner.

- If you miss the bank shot, simply adjust your aim.

### Chain Reaction

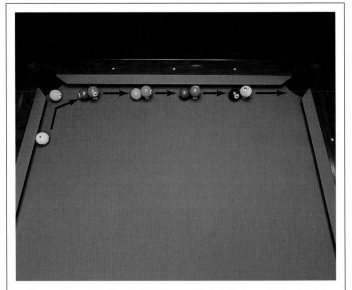

- Place the cue ball and 1 ball as shown.

- Using a one-ball gap, place the 2 ball one chalk's width from the short rail.

- Put a chalk under the 3 and freeze the 2 ball to it. Use a three-ball gap and do the same thing to the

- 4, 5, 6, 7, 8, and 9 balls. Put chalk under the 3, 5, 7, and 9 balls.

- Shoot the 1 ball into the corner, and the cue ball will carom into the 2, starting a chain reaction. The 9 will go into the corner pocket.

I will develop a trick shot using it." After all, no matter what the prop is, you either have to hit it, go over it, go under it, go through it, or go around or in it. The only thing holding you back is your imagination.

Caution: When looking for a prop, be sure to avoid using glass or other breakable objects. During one televised event, a player used glasses during his trick shot. It was all good until another player hit a shot too hard, and the broken glass went flying all over the table. Instead, start off by using props such as wood, hard plastic, or cushions.

## Tee It Up

- Place the 2 and the 3 balls about 6 inches from the side pocket, frozen and parallel with the long rail.

- Place two tees upright as shown. Freeze the 1 and 9 balls to the 2 and 3 balls as shown.

- You want to place the cue ball about 1 foot away from the 1 ball.

- Shoot the cue ball into the 1 ball, making the 9 in the side without knocking down the tees.

## Coin in the Glass

- The object of this shot is to shoot into the 5 ball, which will cause the dime to jump into the shot glass.

- Place the shot glass on the rail as shown. Place the dime about one-half inch from the edge of the cushion.

- Freeze the 5 ball to the cushion in line with the dime and the shot glass.

- Take the cue ball and shoot into the 5 with medium speed. You may have to adjust your speed.

# YOU CAN DO THIS

## With just a bit of time and practice, everyone can do these crowd pleasers

These next four shots are a bit more difficult than the previous ones, but you can make them. The first shot is right from the movie *Pool Hall Junkies*. It is a timing shot that may actually come up in a game, minus the rack, of course. When this shot was invented, no doubt it came up in a game, and someone decided to make a trick shot out of it.

Again we have added a few props to these shots. If you find yourself in a situation where you are unable to make a shot, try adding the prop. A rack is a great way to make a shot easier. You will have a much larger target to shoot at. Remember that you want to make the shot. If you attempt a shot and the toughest part of the shot goes in, but you miss the easier

### *It's 8 Ball Time*

- The object of this shot is to play the 8 ball in the near side pocket.

- Freeze the cue ball and the 8 ball to the cushion and each other at the first diamond as shown.

- Place the rack as shown.

- Aim the cue ball at the center of the far side pocket. The 8 ball will hit the rack, and the cue ball will kick back and pocket the 8 in the side.

### *One for the Money*

- You want to pocket the 9 ball into the far left corner.

- Place the 9 on the second diamond, frozen to the cushion. Freeze the 1, 2, and 3 to the 9 ball as shown.

- The cue ball is placed about 1 foot from the 1 ball as shown.

- Shoot directly into the 1 ball with a medium hard stroke. Make adjustments by moving the cluster up or down the rail as needed.

part, the audience will remember only the ball you missed. So, never hesitate to use a rack, bridge, or extra balls to make your shot easier.

These shots will become easy for you to make, and your audience will love them. Become good and consistent at each trick. If you struggle with a certain shot, don't use it when you are entertaining. All trick shot players have their favorite shots, and they also have a list of shots that they just do not like to play. When they entertain or compete, they avoid the shots that they are not fully confident of.

## *Through the Woods*

- Place the 1 ball near the corner pocket. Place the rack about 2 feet from the 1 ball as shown.

- Place the cue ball about 1 foot from the rack in a straight line with the 1 ball.

- Elevate your cue about 30 degrees. Aim your cue a half tip below the center on the cue ball. Shoot with a punch stroke with medium hard speed.

- The cue ball will elevate slightly and go over the rack and pocket the ball.

## *Crazy 8 Ball*

- For this shot you will need to buy an 8 ball that is weighted to one side.

- Place the crazy 8 ball on the rail about 6 inches from the side pocket. Place the weighted side toward the cushion.

- Surround the side pocket with blocker balls.

- Put the cue ball about 6 inches away from the crazy 8. Hit this shot soft and watch as it disappears into the side pocket.

# TAKING THE NEXT STEP

## After you have learned basic trick shots, it is time to move up to intermediate shots

It's time to graduate to some trickier shots. Some of these shots require a few more skills than the beginner ones. They also require more time to perfect.

When shooting trick shots, everything is legal, and just about anything goes. Some shots require you to keep the tip on the cue ball and push it. This would not be legal in

regular games of pool such as 8-Ball or Straight Pool, but in trick shots, it is good. The first time most players attempt these strokes, they feel strange and take some getting used to. But after you have practiced them enough times, they will become easy.

You may recognize some of these shots from televised

### The 3-2-1 Shot

- You need to hit the 3, 2, and 1 balls in that order and pocket them in the correct order: 1, 2, and 3.

- Place the 2 ball on the head spot. Put the 1 and 3 balls one diamond away on the head string.

- Hit the 3 ball first at soft speed. Hit the 2 ball next at medium speed and finally the 1 ball at maximum speed.

- The balls will pass each other and go into the pocket in the correct order.

### Easy as 1, 2, 3, 4

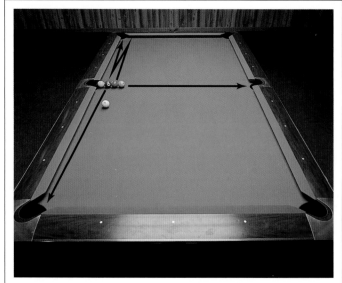

- Place the 1, 2, 3, and 4 balls straight out from the side pocket.

- The cue ball is the third ball out from the rail at the first diamond.

- Hit the cue ball at four o'clock. Hit the 3 ball thin on left side and carom into

- the 2 ball with medium hard speed.

- All four balls will go in: the 1 ball in the side pocket, the 2 in the far corner. The 3 will bank to the near corner, and the 4 will go into the opposite side pocket.

events. Many of them were created by the players participating in these events, whereas other shots have been around for a long time.

The illustrations will help you set up and make these shots. They show you exactly where you need to place the balls. Some shots do not require the balls to be put in an exact position, and you have some leeway, whereas other shots are very precise in their setup. Again, adjustments to the shots may be necessary. When you miss a shot, especially a multiple-ball shot, you need to know where the ball missed.

Did it miss to the right of the pocket or the left? By knowing this, you can make the proper adjustments. It is always helpful to have someone watch to let you know where the ball missed.

## Miss 'em All

- The object is to hit the cue ball past the first blocker ball and go two more rails without touching the other two blocker balls. You must keep the cue ball "inside the kitchen."

- Place three balls on the rails as shown in the picture. The balls are on the diamonds.

- Hit the cue ball with a draw stroke at six o'clock. Shoot easy!

- You want the cue ball sliding as it hits the first rail.

## Hustler Bank

- Freeze the 8 ball to the cushion about 2 inches from the corner pocket.

- Freeze the cue ball to the 8, straight out.

- Aim straight into the 8 ball with extreme high using an open bridge. You need just a touch of right English.

- With a medium stroke, follow through and let the tip glance upward so it clears out of the way for the 8 ball to bank.

159

# AS SEEN ON TV

## You may have seen one of these shots in a commercial many years ago

Back in the 1970s Steve Mizerak filmed a Miller Lite commercial and made one trick shot very famous which later became known as "The just showing off shot". The shot was named after his last quote in the commercial. Even today it is rare that you find an amateur pool player who hasn't heard of this shot. It is definitely a crowd favorite because you make

five balls in four different pockets, and the cue ball finishes the shot off by traveling around the table to pocket the last couple of balls. Filming this shot for the commercial required 181 takes.

The second shot was featured in the movie *The Color of Money*, released in the 1980s. It is a kiss-back shot in which

### *Just Showing Off Set Up*

- This shot pockets seven balls into five pockets. Setup is critical.

- The 1 ball is frozen to the cushion about one chalk's width from the pocket point. The 2 ball is frozen straight out from the 1 ball.

- The 3 and 4 balls are also straight across, just slightly past the center of the side pocket.

- The 5 ball is placed as shown and aimed just past the corner pocket point on the long rail.

### *Shooting the Just Showing Off*

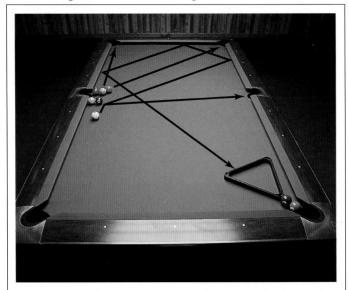

- Place the cue ball on the third diamond line about one ball's width from the cushion.

- Hit the cue ball with high left English and aim to cut the 2 ball into the side pocket.

- After contacting the 2 ball, the cue ball should hit the long rail near the first diamond.

- The high left English will help the cue ball travel three rails, hit the rack, and pocket the two balls in the corner.

you actually shoot into the cushion and cause the 8 ball to travel down the long rail and into the corner pocket. Paul Newman was taught this shot by technical advisor Mike Sigel, but Paul Newman actually was able to perform this shot on camera.

Moving to today, you may have seen this last shot performed on television by some of the more recent trick shot artists. Even some of the older shots have been slightly modified for today's TV audience. In fact, many of the trick shots in this book have been used in TV shows and commercials.

Movie directors often like to put a trick shot into a pool scene. Some of the top trick shot artists of today have been called to either shoot the shot or to show an actor how to make it. So, the next time you go to the movies and see a trick shot, most likely one of the top professional players was involved.

## The Color of Money *Shot*

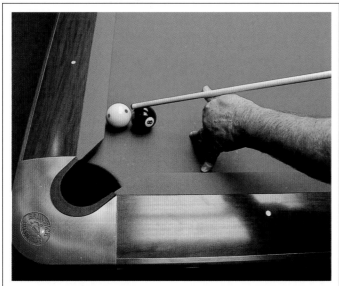

- This is a legal shot that may even come up in a game.

- The cue ball is frozen to the cushion, and the 8 ball is frozen to the cue ball.

- The balls are lined up directly at the corner pocket.

- Using an open bridge and shooting over the 8 ball, hit the cue ball with high English. The 8 ball will kick back and go into the corner pocket, leaving the cue ball where it is.

## *Three-rail Reverse*

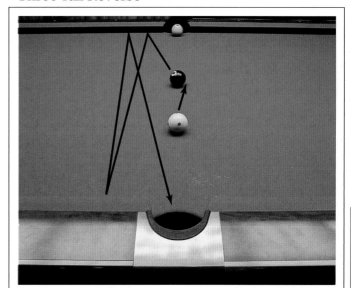

- This is another shot that you could use to win a game.

- All three balls are lined up on the center of the table as shown. The 8 ball is dead center, and the cue ball is about one diamond away.

- Shoot with a firm center ball stroke and have the 8 ball just miss the side pocket and blocking ball.

- The 8 ball will bank back and forth three rails and go into the side pocket closest to you.

# ONE & DONE

## These shots involve pocketing only one ball; knowledge is the key to making them

You don't have to pocket multiple balls for the shot to be entertaining. In many shots you pocket only one ball, and your audience will be amazed. When you are shooting these shots, take your time to explain where the ball is going to be pocketed. Doing this is important. Some players have groups of balls on the table and try to pocket just one ball.

When they shoot the shot and make it, the audience members are disappointed because they thought all the balls would go in.

During televised events players are required to use props during 80 percent of their shots. When you pocket a single ball, props can be helpful in making the shot look better.

### Jump Bank Shot

- The 8 ball is blocked from banking cross side.

- All three balls are about two balls' width from the cushion and about 1 inch apart.

- The cue ball is lined up to have a straight bank shot on the 8 ball.

- Shoot down on the cue ball to cause it to jump slightly. When it impacts the 8 ball, it will jump as well, hit the rail, and fly over the two balls into the other side pocket.

### Squeeze Shot

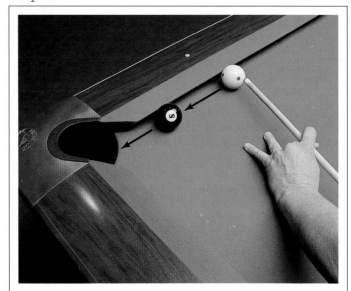

- The 8 ball is about one chalk's width from the pocket point and slightly off the cushion (about ⅛ inch).

- The cue ball is frozen to the cushion near the first diamond.

- Aim directly into the rail and first place your tip on the cue ball slightly right of center. After the tip is touching the cue ball, simply push through the cue ball and have it squirt to the left to pocket the 8 ball.

Even a difficult shot in which only one ball goes in sometimes looks better with a prop.

Many shots started with only one ball being pocketed, but players have found ways to add to them to make the tricks look more spectacular. This is how many trick shots that start as simple ones become more difficult.

On televised events, players are given only two attempts to make the shot, whereas in regular tour events players get three attempts. When a player starts missing the multiple-ball tricks, he usually goes to a single-ball trick. You have much more control over one ball going in than several balls. This also is true if you are entertaining your friends. If you find yourself missing a couple of shots in a row, you should go to a single-ball shot that you have confidence in.

## Compression Shot

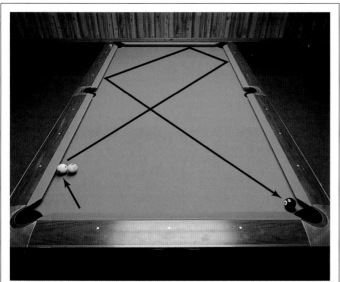

- The cue ball and object ball are at the first diamond, with the cue ball frozen to the rail.

- The 8 ball is hanging by the corner.

- Your cue stick should be aiming near one and one-half diamonds on the long rail.

- With slight center-left English, shoot the cue ball and compress the rail, allowing the ball to escape and go three rails to pocket the 8 ball, winning the game.

## Compression Kick Shot

- This is another compression shot.

- The cue ball is frozen to the rail at the second diamond. The other balls are frozen and form a right angle.

- Aim the cue stick at about two and one-half diamonds.

- With a firm center ball hit, shoot the cue ball and compress the rail. The cue ball will escape and kick the 8 ball into the side pocket. Be sure to use a poke stroke to avoid hitting the blocker ball.

# MORE TRICKS OF THE TRADE
## Master these to entertain friends and family

Players come up with many great trick shots. You can find a wide variety of videos of trick shots on the Internet. The popularity of trick shots has soared in recent years. Many people who watch the pros on television attempt to make the same shots on their own table. Then they get creative and add their own little twists and turns to them.

Every trick shot artist develops the type of shot that he feels most comfortable with, whether it is a jump, massé, draw,

or stroke. You should do the same. Find your strengths and design shots that work well with them. It is fun to create shots. Sometimes it is as simple as designing a shot around an item in your home. This is how many of the shots on television were developed.

You can do a shot that includes two types of shots. Break the shot down into two parts. For example, you may want to hit a stroke shot and quickly follow it up with a jump. You can

### Cut It Thin to Win

- The object balls are on the long center line of the table.

- The 1 ball is two balls' width from the center spot.

- The 1 ball is frozen to the 2 ball.

- Shoot into the 1 ball, cutting it very thin, almost (but not quite) directly into the 2 ball. You need to use a lot of draw.

- You need to use a lot of draw. The cue ball causes the 1 ball to push to the left and go into the side pocket.

### Cue Ball Makes Four

- The 4 ball is on the spot, and the 3 ball is frozen to it (above the spot), lined up at the long rail pocket point.

- The cue ball is near the side pocket.

- The 1 and 2 balls are frozen to the cue ball, lined up as indicated.

- Using a center ball hit, aim the cue ball about half a ball's width to the left of the 3 ball. Shoot firmly to make all four balls.

even add a massé. These types of shots require more time and concentration. Changing over from a draw stroke to a massé stroke can be difficult. But it will make the shot look that much more impressive. Try it and see if you can do it. Break the shot down into parts, learning them one at a time. Then put all the parts together.

## Hand Is Faster than the Eye

- The cue ball, 8 ball, and 9 ball are all lined up directly into the corner pocket.

- The 8 ball is on the spot, and the others are as shown.

- Hit the cue ball with a long follow-through stroke. The cue and 1 ball get out of the way.

- The tip of the cue stick will hit the 8 ball into the 9 ball, pocketing it.

## Carom Draw Shot

- The cue ball is on the 3 x 1 diamond intersection line.

- The 1 ball is even with the cue ball, one diamond away.

- The 2 and 3 balls are hanging as shown.

- Hit the cue ball with maximum draw, cutting the 1 ball slightly. The cue ball caroms to the right, pocketing the 2 ball and drawing back to make the 3 ball. Adjust your aim on the first ball to get the carom just right.

# OLDIES BUT GOODIES

## The butterfly shot has been around for so long that no one knows who invented it

A popular trick shot, second only to the "Just Showing Off" shot, is the butterfly shot. The butterfly shot has been around for so long that no one knows when or by whom it was invented. What makes the shot so spectacular is that six balls go into six different pockets. This is not easy to do. In an expanded variation of this shot, call the "Titanic Shot," players attempt to pocket fifteen balls in one stroke. The nice part of the Titanic Shot is that, if some of the balls don't go into the pockets, you can simply remind your audience that the *Titanic* had survivors.

Some old books show the trick shots that players shot years ago. The creativity of these artists was truly amazing. They

### Butterfly Shot Set Up

- The setup of this shot is critical in order to make it. Lay your cue stick on the table, lined up with the end diamonds.

- At three and one-half diamonds, place a ball on both sides of the cue stick.

- Two balls should have a little more than a half-ball gap between them.

- Freeze two more balls to each of the first two balls and aim them at the four corner pockets.

### Shooting the Butterfly Shot

- The end balls must be aimed at the outside edge of the corner pockets.

- Place the cue ball so that it is directly in line with the gap between the middle balls. Use a center ball hit on the cue ball.

- With a stroke that is level and firm but not too hard, hit the cue ball at the gap.

- All six balls will go into six pockets. You may have to make adjustments, depending on the table.

did not have the benefit of YouTube or even television to see other players shoot these shots. They had to either create them by themselves or learn from another player.

In the 1980s made-for-television pool events in Atlantic City, New Jersey, showcased the legends of pool, including Willie Mosconi, Luther Lassiter, Minnesota Fats, and Irving Crane. After their regular pool event was completed, the players would shoot their favorite trick shots. They all were good at them because when they did exhibitions, the audience would always ask the players to show off their best trick shots. These players helped to pave the way for the trick shot artists of today. You can see some of these events on ESPN classics.

## Squeeze Jump Shot

- Place six blocker balls in a semicircle as shown near the corner pocket with the 1 ball at the first diamond.

- Place the 8 ball hanging near the jaws of the corner.

- Place the cue ball one ball's gap to the left of the 1 ball.

- Place your tip on the cue ball at about seven o'clock. Push your stick through the cue ball. The cue ball will jump into the air and make the 8.

## Get Out of the Way

- Place three balls along the long rail at the first, second, and third diamonds. The 9 ball needs to be slightly off the rail as shown.

- Place the cue ball at the first diamond past the side rail and a two-ball gap out from the rail.

- With high English, aim your tip at the middle of the first object ball (1 ball).

- The two blocking balls will clear out, and the cue ball will pocket the 9.

# SPEED & ACCURACY
## You need to shoot quickly and precisely in a trick shot tournament

Wing shots are both great trick shots and a great way to warm up quickly before an event. Warming up helps both in trick shots and in regular games of pool. They are fast-paced shots that require much practice. What makes the shots so difficult is that you are shooting at a moving target. It is hard enough to pocket a ball the length of the table, but when it is moving, the shot is much more difficult.

Perhaps the best present-day master of these types of shots is Tom Rossman, also known as "Dr. Cue." He practices these shots every day. Considering his wins at *Trick Shot Magic* and many top finishes, they are a sure way to improve your game. Wing shots seem difficult when you start out because your brain is actually thinking too much. You need to shoot these shots with feel. If you think about the shot as you stroke the cue, you will not make it. You must be relaxed and just let it happen. Practice these shots as much as you can, and you

### Wing Shot Set Up

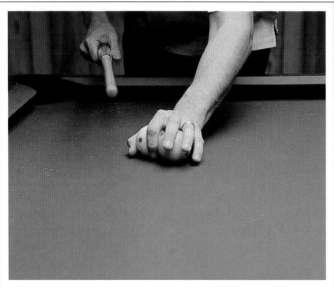

- Hold the cue ball and the object ball in the same hand.

- You want to let the object ball roll down the table while you still have the cue ball in your hand.

- Try to maintain the same speed each time.

- Aim the object ball to roll in the same place each time for better consistency.

- Quickly place the cue ball down behind the head string and prepare to shoot.

### Shooting the Wing Shot

- After placing the cue ball down, you must quickly get into the shooting position.

- This shot does not give you much time to think, so you are relying on instinct. You must be ready to shoot right away.

- Keep your eye on the object ball when shooting.

- Let the shot happen, and you will be surprised by how many of these shots you can make.

will soon start making them with consistency.

You also get warmed up in a hurry at any event by shooting wing shots. They get the blood flowing and relax the mind, creating the perfect combination for playing great pool. Give them a try. And if you run into Dr. Cue, ask him how much these shots have helped to make him one of the top trick shot performers today.

## What Happened?

- Place three balls as shown (2, 3, and 9). Put the 7 and 8 balls at an angle, frozen together at the last diamond.

- The cue ball is a one-ball gap from the cushion at the first diamond. Freeze the 1 ball to the cue ball and have them lined up at the first ball (2).

- Aim the cue ball at the side pocket, just beyond the 9.

- Using center ball, shoot the cue ball, all the balls will clear as the 9 goes into the corner

## Speed Shot

- This shot requires both speed and accuracy. Place four balls on the rail as shown.

- The gap is one ball between each of the three balls. The 4 ball is placed at the third diamond.

- Hit the 4 ball softly toward the corner pocket. Hurry over to the 1, 2, and 3 balls and quickly shoot them into the same corner pocket.

- The balls must go in order, with the 4 ball going in last.

# SKILLED SHOTS
## These are the shots you have probably seen at televised events

The shots listed in this chapter are difficult and take dedication and practice to make on a consistent basis. Many of these shots require a much different stroke than you are use to. As a matter of fact, one of these shots requires you to hold the cue stick near the joint. And then to hit the shot, you must use the palm of your hand and slap at the stick.

It was at *Trick Shot Magic* that Mike Massey came up with a shot that changed the game of trick shots forever. Mike

placed a cowboy boot 11 feet away and jumped a cue ball off the table and into the boot. After its debut on ESPN, the shot took on a life of its own. People request "the Boot Shot" everywhere Mike performs. He has performed that shot everywhere, including on *Live with Regis and Kelly* and *The Best Damn Sports Show* with Tom Arnold.

The Internet has opened up a new world of trick shots. Some shots showcased online are unbelievable. Players from

### *Six-ball Speed Shot*

- Line up six object balls on the first diamond, evenly spread apart.

- The 8 ball is located on the first diamond, even with the side pocket as shown.

- Shoot the 8 ball first, slowly toward the corner pocket. While it is rolling, quickly shoot the other six balls into the same pocket.

- The object balls should all be made in the corner pocket before the 8 ball.

### *Karate Chop Shot*

- You can't reach this draw shot, so you need to lay the cue stick on the table.

- Grab it with two fingers near the joint, lifting it off the table slightly.

- The tip should be no more than 1 inch away from the cue ball and about one-quarter inch off the table.

- Your other hand will be palm forward, and you will slap the butt end to drive the cue stick forward and into the cue ball.

all over the world are inventing new shots everyday. Shots are being created using two or more pool tables where the cue ball jumps from one table to the next and pockets balls. One of the most amazing videos is of a player who sets up dominoes on three tables. The dominoes are lined up perfectly to make numerous balls go into pockets as the dominos fall. The entire shot takes about four minutes.

The imagination is the endless when it comes to creating trick shots. Just a few years back, no one would have thought of shooting a one handed jump shot, never mind left and right handed, or how about the triple jump where players jump three balls with three cues at one time. It just keeps getting better and better. Keep practicing and never be afraid to try something new

## Jimmy Moore Draw Shot

- Only a handful of players in the world shoot this shot with any consistency.

- The 1 ball is almost a straight shot (slight angle) into the corner pocket.

- After you shoot the 1 ball, the cue ball will carom into the cushion on the other side of the 8 ball, kick back out, and then draw down around the 8 ball, pocketing the 9 ball.

- You need to hit this with a lot of draw and very little right English.

## Mike Massey Boot Shot

- This shot was made famous in 2003 on ESPN by Mike Massey.

- The distance between the cue ball and cowboy boot is about 11 feet.

- The boot is propped up at an angle so the opening is facing the shooter.

- This is a power jump with accuracy. It is a shot you will need to practice so you can find the distance that allows you to jump the cue ball into the boot.

# STROKE & JUMP

## Two of these shots require a great stroke, and the other two require a great jump

These next four shots have all been shown on ESPN. To perform these shots you need to have a good stroke. Mike Massey showed the fouette shot to one of the best 9-Ball pool players in the world. After a couple of hours of failed attempts to make the shot, the player gave up. This is not to say that professional pool players can't do trick shots. To

the contrary, they would be good trick shot artists in a short period of time. They already have a great stroke, and they understand all the concepts involved with throw and tangent lines.

Bruce Barthelette came up with the baseball glove and stacker shot (below) about six years ago as he prepared for

### Green Monster Shot

- This shot was created in 2005 at the ESPN *Trick Shot Magic* event. It was named after the Green Monster wall at Fenway Park in Boston.

- The Green Monster is 9½ inches high and is located at two and one-half diamonds.

- You really need to use all your power on this shot. The cue ball will travel 9 feet in the air and land in the glove. A long stroke with a loose grip using a jump cue is required.

### Fouette Shot

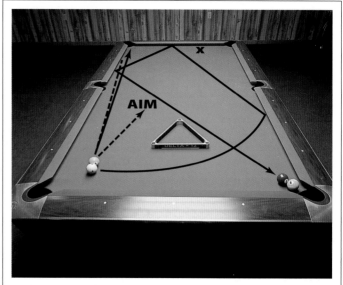

- The cue ball is about a two-ball gap off the rail and at the half diamond. The one ball is about one-half inch from the cue ball.

- Place the 2 and 9 balls and the rack as shown.

- Line up the cue ball and 1 ball to the left inside edge

of the corner pocket.

- Elevate the butt of your cue slightly and hit the cue ball at 10:30 o'clock. Hit firmly and follow through. The cue ball will curve around the rack and go three or four rails to make the combination.

172

his first ESPN *Trick Shot Magic* event. His good friend Sal Conti helped him design shots for the competition. He had an idea for a shot that involved a baseball glove. One thing led to another, and the "Green Monster Shot" was created in honor of his favorite baseball team, the Boston Red Sox.

The stacker shot had not been done before. It involved being quick and being able to jump. Combining speed and jump made the shot difficult for his opponents to make.

## Jump to Stacker Shot Setup

- This shot requires both speed and jump.

- Put the special stacker 8 ball in the corner pocket. The stacker ball has a flat bottom and also a small hole on top so that the other 8 ball can balance on it.

- Place the regulation 8 ball on top of the stacker ball.

- Line the two cue balls up for the corner pocket. Use about a three-quarter inch gap.

## Shooting the Jump to Stacker Shot

- Hit the first cue ball into the second cue ball, sending it toward the object balls.

- Quickly hit a jump shot and make the first cue ball go over the second cue ball.

- The second cue ball will pocket the bottom 8 ball, and the first cue ball will pocket the top ball.

- The top 8 ball will drop down after the bottom one has been made.

# JUMPS & MASSÉS

## These shots require a controlled jump shot and some difficult massé shots

Shooting these trick shots is both challenging and rewarding. Nobody can just walk up to a table and start making these shots without a tremendous amount of practicing. The players who perform these trick shots are, in a way, like magicians. Certain shots entail secrets that make them much easier to execute. The players are generous in sharing their knowledge. Pool is one sport in which just about everyone helps anyone who asks. This is one of the reasons why trick shot players have become so good so quickly.

Trick shot players tend to be audience-friendly. They are used to performing in front of crowds and making people smile. Overall it's a fun, welcoming atmosphere. And, win or

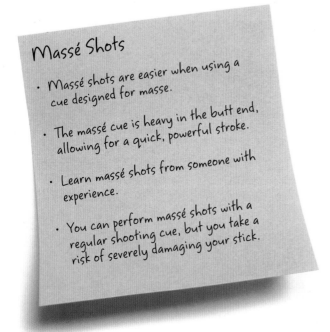

## Massé Shots

- Massé shots are easier when using a cue designed for masse.

- The massé cue is heavy in the butt end, allowing for a quick, powerful stroke.

- Learn massé shots from someone with experience.

- You can perform massé shots with a regular shooting cue, but you take a risk of severely damaging your stick.

*Rainbow Massé Shot*

- This is a difficult shot that will curve the cue ball around a row of balls in the shape of a rainbow or half moon.

- Place the balls as shown in the picture.

- The cue ball is located at the 1 X 1 diamond.

- Hold the cue stick so it is almost vertical. Hit the cue ball at 7:30. If you miss to the right, try seven o'clock on the cue ball or get more vertical.

lose, the opponents always congratulate each other at the end of the match. With all of this excitement and genuine love for the sport, it's no wonder that ESPN *Trick Shot Magic* and the *World Cup of Trick Shots* are the highest-rated televised pool events.

If you want to learn these shots, play in a tournament and talk to those who have been executing these shots for years. It is the fastest way to gain the knowledge necessary to make these shots.

## Minguad Massé Shot

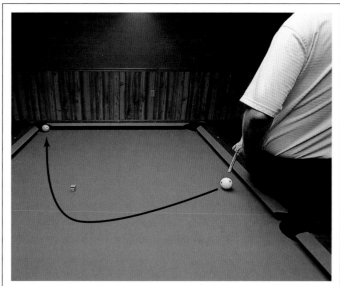

- Start with a three o'clock hit on the cue ball. You may have to adjust and go to 3:30 or even four o'clock, depending on your stroke.

- This shot requires a quick punch stroke.

- Aim far enough to the left of the chalk to allow for squirt.

- This is a difficult shot because it requires the correct amount of English and speed.

## Jump Massé Out of Rack

- You need a hard tip to make this shot.

- Your cue needs to be positioned straight up and down.

- Hit the cue ball at six o'clock with a hard stroke. You need to pinch the cue ball so it will jump out of the

rack with lots of backspin on it.

- The cue ball will go up table and draw back to pocket the object ball.

175

# MORE GREAT SHOTS

## Just when you thought you had seen it all, along comes a shot using three jump cues at once

One of the most exciting world championship trick shot tournaments took place in St. Petersburg, Russia, in 2007. Top players from all over the world attended. The final match came down to Andy "the Magic Man" Segal of the United States and Sebastian "the Matador" Giumelli of Argentina. Giumelli led most of the way, but Andy Segal

put on a late charge. With one shot left in the match, Segal would have to make the Yo Yo massé on his first attempt to tie Giumelli and send the match into a playoff. Segal went up to the table and hit the shot perfectly on his first attempt to tie Giumelli. Now the title of world champion came down to one playoff shot.

### Great Escape Shot

- The photo above shows Andy Segal, the number one trick shot artist in the world, demonstrating the shot.

- Using your normal playing cue, aim your tip into the rail at the half diamond with top-left English.

- You need a quick stroke on this shot.

- The cue ball will come off the short rail, hit the long rail, and curve around the 2 ball to make the 1-9 combination shot.

### Two-millimeter Shot

- This shot requires a good stroke. The cue ball and the 1 ball have spacing of 2 millimeters.

- The 1 ball is going to draw around the 8 ball and pocket the 9 ball in the far corner.

- You need to hit this shot at 5:30 o'clock on the cue ball.

- Let the cue stick follow on through when you shoot. The cue ball will go sideways and then draw back to make the 9 ball.

Both players lagged to see who would have the choice of shooting first or second. Segal won the lag and elected to go second. The playoff shot required the players to hit three balls and make a three-, four-, and five-rail bank shot. Each player was allowed one attempt. Giumelli went up first and was unable to make any of the bank shots. All Segal needed to win was to make any one of the bank shots. He made two of the three banks shots in one of the most exciting finishes in trick shot history.

## Triple Jump

- The hardest part of this shot is holding the three cue sticks at once. Dave Nangle invented this shot.

- Get a good grip on the three jump cues.

- You need to have all three tips of the cues at approximately the same distance from each object ball.

- A firm stroke is needed to make all three balls jump and go into the corner pocket. The rack will act as a guide to pocket the balls.

## Yo Yo Massé

- This is a power massé shot. Put the 8 ball near the side pocket as shown.

- The cue ball is at the second diamond. Aim your tip at 6:30 on the clock on the cue ball with the cue stick almost vertical.

- Hit straight down, and the cue ball will go up table past the side pocket.

- The English will grab, drawing the cue ball back to pocket the 8 ball in the side.

ADVANCED TRICK SHOTS

# ANOTHER GREAT FINISH
## Every trick shot player wants the title of world champion

In December 2008 the best trick shot artists from around the globe participated in the World Artistic Pool Championship in Atlanta, Georgia. The stage was set for some spectacular shooting with former world champions in the field, including Andy Segal, Charles Darling, and Tom "Dr. Cue" Rossman. Other notables in the field had made their claim on television, including Bruce Barthelette, Nick Nikolaidis, Ralph Eckert, and Eric Yow. Other great hopefuls were also in attendance.

At the conclusion of the preliminary rounds, there was no surprise as Segal and Rossman earned the top two seeds and secured a first-round playoff bye. The third and fourth seeds were earned by Gabi Visoiu and Jamey "Sharpshooter" Gray.

The quarter-final round of the playoffs was intense as Gray squared off against Nikolaidis, who had just defeated Segal, the reigning world champion. Gray managed to defeat Nikolaidis on a dramatic final shot and scored 111 points to

### Prison Shot

- Jump the cue ball out of two racks and make the 8 ball. Jamey Gray came up with this shot for the *Trick Shot Magic* event. This is one of the most difficult shots.

- You need an extremely light jump cue to get the necessary height.

- Aim the tip at six o'clock and hit down on the cue ball very hard.

- The cue ball will jump almost straight up into the air, clear the racks, and make the 8 ball.

### Two One-hand Jumps

- Line up two rows of balls as shown with about a two-ball gap between the rows of balls.

- With a jump cue in each hand, jump the back row of balls over the front row into the corner pocket.

- Start with the right hand and keep switching with each jump until all five balls have gone in.

- Hold the jump cues with a light grip. Practice by lining up fifteen balls and jumping over a piece of wood.

Nikolaidis's 109. On the other side of the bracket, Tom Rossman edged out Eric Yow with a score of 110–99 points.

The finals were in the hands of veteran Rossman and young gun Gray. At the conclusion of the intense back-and-forth battle, the world championship came down to one shot. Rossman chose an incredible five-rail kick shot to cut an object into the corner pocket, hanging for just a moment before going in and causing the crowd to roar. Gray took a moment to let the crowd settle and to muster his composure. He approached the table with fire in his heart and the steady hands of a sharpshooter and fired the cue ball five rails, sending the object ball straight into the pocket with no hesitation or doubt. Jamey Gray had just earned the title of world champion.

## Jump Beat Shot Setup

- The object of this shot is to make the cue ball jump just enough to catch the top of the 8 ball.

- Both balls will go into the corner pocket, with the cue ball going in first.

- You want the cue ball and the 8 ball in line with the corner pocket.

- The gap will depend on how much you can jump the cue ball. Start with a two-ball gap and adjust from there.

## Shooting the Jump Beat Shot

- Using a jump cue, slightly elevate the butt end of the cue.

- Use a light grip on the cue. Hit the cue ball just below center.

- The cue ball will hit the top of the 8 ball and get it rolling toward the corner pocket.

- The cue ball will go into the corner pocket first, followed by the 8 ball.

# MORE TELEVISION SHOTS
## You have seen these shots on TV; now you will know how to make them

The knowledge of how to make trick shots has been passed from one player to another. But knowledge is only the first step. To become a good trick shot player, you need dedication and practice. The more you practice and the better your stroke, the better chance you have of making these shots.

After you have mastered these difficult shots, you can entertain your friends and family. You will need to put in the time and effort, but they are worth it.

If you are serious about trick shots, enter a tournament. It is the best way to get your feet wet and learn at the same time. A tournament is always a great experience for players. If you have any questions, someone at the event will be happy to

### Sebastian Fouette Shot Setup

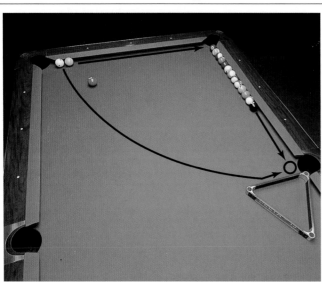

- Line up thirteen balls on the rail and frozen together.

- The middle of the 6 ball is even with the point in the corner pocket.

- Put the cue ball near the corner pocket and frozen to the rail with about one-quarter-inch gap from the 1 ball as shown.

- Place the rack in the side pocket as shown. Place a blocker at the first diamond and the fifth ball out from the rail.

### Shooting the Sebastian Fouette Shot

- Aim your cue at the first diamond on the long rail. Hit the cue ball at eleven o'clock.

- The 1 ball will go into the corner pocket and also hit the 6 ball, which will send the 8 ball up the long rail.

- The 8 ball will sit in front of the side pocket.

- The cue ball will curve around the blocker ball and pocket the 8 in the side.

help you out. After all, everyone started the same way: as a new player.

The three shots described in this section have all been played on television. The fouette shot in the first two pictures was invented by Sebastian Giumelli of Argentina. Sebastian has created many of the great shots that you have seen on television.

## Wall of Balls

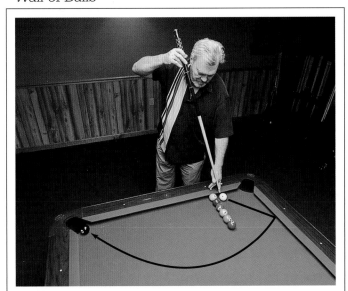

- Line up six balls on the first diamond as shown.

- Place the cue ball about one chalk's width from the rail and one chalk's width from the first ball.

- Holding the cue stick at the angle shown, aim your tip to hit the cue ball at 6:30. Aim at one and a half diamonds on the long rail.

- A medium but firm stroke is needed. The cue ball will go around the wall of balls and pocket the 8 ball into the corner.

## Over/Under

- Place the bridge across the table at the first diamond. Place the cue ball and 1 ball about one ball's width from the rail.

- Place the 1 ball so that the leading edge is even with the bridge.

- Holding your playing cue with a light grip and slightly elevated, hit the cue ball at six o'clock with a firm stroke.

- The cue ball will go over the bridge and draw back to make the 9.

181

# PRESHOT PRACTICE

## Good form and fundamentals will enable you to make more shots and improve your overall performance

For optimal performance, you should develop a preshot routine. A preshot routine is just as important as the shot itself.

When you are a beginner, you may be learning proper fundamentals from the start or correcting your fundamentals. More-experienced players should need only minor adjustments to fine-tune theirs. Practice with a partner so he can help you

make adjustments in your form and your approach to the table.

You should be comfortable, but you should realize that you may not be when you first start correcting your form. When you make an adjustment, it takes time to get used to. Additionally, one small adjustment may lead to another.

Walking into your shot, staying in line with your shot,

### Preshot Routine

- You will develop a rhythm when you have a preshot routine.

- Your preshot routine should include chalking up your cue before or after each shot and walking around the table before you address a ball.

- Analyze your options and the table layout to find a pattern that works for you.

- Consistency is a good thing. If you stick to the same habits before each shot, you will find your rhythm.

### Walk into Your Shot

- When you address the ball, walk into your shot and get down in line with it. Your goal is to minimize stance adjustments.

- Step into the shot and guide your cue stick toward the cue ball. Some players keep their cue stick at

their side when they step forward.

- Some players lay their cue on the table in front of them first.

- Others step into the shot as though the cue stick is an extension of their arm.

executing practice strokes for cueing the ball, and looking back and forth among the cue, object ball, and the pocket are all habits to incorporate into your game as your preshot routine.

When you find yourself making excessive adjustments while down on your shot, you should get up and repeat your preshot process. Lack of attention to this step can often cause you to miss your shot.

A preshot routine will help you get into a rhythm that works for you. When you develop consistent habits, you will ultimately improve your results.

## Practice Strokes

- After you are in position to address the cue ball, you should do practice strokes.

- Three to five practice strokes are an average amount. You should do what feels best for you.

- You should maintain consistency and use the same number of practice strokes for each shot.

- Much more than the average amount or an inconsistent amount of practice strokes may cause you to miss a shot.

## Stay Down

- Jumping up can create cueing errors that result in missed shots. A good way to tell if you are jumping up is to have a friend hold a hand above your back.

- It is important to stay down on your shot all the way through your stroke.

- Listen for the sound of the ball dropping into the pocket instead of watching it.

- You may not be able to stay down that long; therefore, after your follow-through stroke is completed, you may get up.

# CONTROLLING THE CUE BALL

## If you learn to control the cue ball, you can become a more powerful player

Cue ball control drills help you get a feel for your stroke and improve your position play. You can do various exercises to determine your speed and shooting style. Start by using the center ball axis with follow, center, and draw. Vary your stroke speeds using soft, medium soft, medium, or medium hard on each shot. Line your shots up straight and then try

shooting them on an angle or on the rail. Notice the path of the cue ball each time.

In addition to drills, a good practice game for recognizing patterns is to throw the 1 to 9 balls out onto the table and try running them out. You may also play the ghost player. Rack the balls for yourself, break, and then try to run them

### Find Center Ball

- Do this simple exercise to find center ball.

- First set up two object balls 3 inches apart. Place a cube of chalk on the rail between the two object balls.

- Set up the cue ball in line with the chalk. Step into

your stance, aim at the chalk, and shoot.

- If everything is lined up properly and you are contacting center ball, the cue ball will bounce back toward you without disturbing the two object balls.

### Follow

- A good drill for practicing follow is to line up ten object balls in a row straight across the table from one diamond to the opposite diamond.

- Shoot the first five balls in one corner and the other five in the opposite corner with follow.

- Then line up the object balls at the next diamond up and repeat the exercise until you have used all the diamonds.

- The cue ball should be moved along the same line to shoot in each ball.

out. After you miss, the ghost player wins. You can track your progress by the number of balls you run and then graduate to a number of racks as your game improves. These exercises will train you to learn patterns used in different game-play situations. Apply what you learn from cue control drills to achieve your desired position play.

## Draw

- You can line up the balls as in the follow drill and do that same exercise using draw.

- Another good practice for draw is to line up the cue ball and object ball in a straight line in front of a side pocket.

- Shoot the object ball into the side pocket using draw on the cue ball.

- The object is to get the cue ball to come straight back and scratch in the opposite side pocket.

## Stop Shot

- You can also repeat the follow drill using a center ball stop shot instead of follow.

- Another good drill for practicing stop shots is to place a striped ball horizontally near the head spot.

- Then hit the ball with a slightly below-center stroke and shoot it toward the other end.

- Watch the reaction of the object ball as it rolls. Then experiment with different strokes and aiming points.

185

# BANKING PRACTICE

## You should know how to bank a ball to increase your chance to win

Banking is a good skill to learn no matter what game of pool you play. However, you will use banking more in some games than others, such as 9-Ball, One Pocket, and Three-cushion billiards.

Banking practice will help you learn how to shoot angles and how to use banking and kicking systems, like the diamond system, to your advantage. When you practice banks' and come across an opponent who is weaker at banking, you can play to your strengths and his weaknesses. Leave opponents with no choice other than to try for a bank or leave you with a bank shot. Then when they do, you can either bank the ball in a pocket or play a safety.

In some situations banking a ball gives you a better leave on your next ball than if you cut it. When you practice your banking, you can feel confident in going for the shot instead of playing a safety.

### *Equal Distance*

- Set up an object ball an equal distance between the cue ball and a pocket. Use the diamonds to line it up.

- Aim for the object ball to hit the spot on the rail where the midpoint is.

- Shoot the cue ball with a center ball hit directly into the object ball.

- Keep practicing with the same stroke speed until you can make the shot consistently and then try varying your stroke speeds and ball positions.

### *Slide and Roll*

- Set up two bank shots an equal distance apart with one closer to the rail than the other.

- Bank the ball closer to the rail with a soft stroke; it will bank short.

- Bank the ball farther from the rail with a harder stroke; it will drop or come close no matter how hard you hit.

- The ball closer to the rail is still sliding because there is no time for it to begin rolling before it hits.

Practice banking the same shot with varying stroke speeds, and you will learn how much speed affects the angle of the object ball coming off the rail. Also, you will see how slide and roll, angle of approach, and English affect the bank shot. Then practice the same shot with a cut angle or English and notice how the angle changes off the rail. You must take all these factors into account when shooting a bank shot.

You can also use multirail banks in play. Those shots require additional calculations based on the contact point of the rail. The object ball needs to be hit a little harder to bank it the

additional rails. Banking exercises will add knowledge to your repertoire. You can increase your chances of winning.

## *Banking off Equal Distance Line*

- At times the object ball is not lined up an equal distance from the cue ball and the target pocket.

- To bank the ball into the pocket, you need to adjust your angle line.

- Divide the distance from the equal angle and make a line across that adjustment to determine the contact point on the cushion.

- Use a medium stroke.

## *Double Bank*

- In a double bank you hit an object ball into two opposite cushions before it goes into the pocket.

- You want to find the contact point on the first cushion that is an equal distance into the pocket off the second cushion.

- The first contact point would mark a spot at which you would miss the bank short.

- When you apply outside English, the ball will reverse the English after it hits the first cushion and close the angle.

# JUMPING PRACTICE
## Jumping comes in handy when the kick shot is not an option

Jump shots are good to learn just in case you are in a situation in which a kick shot just doesn't cut it. When you know how to jump, you can increase your chances to hit or even make a ball in rather than give your opponent ball-in-hand.

Jumping can be practiced using a normal cue or a jump cue. A jump cue makes it easier to learn these shots, although most leagues do not allow jump cues. Therefore, it is a good idea to learn proper jumping techniques with a normal cue.

It is illegal to jump by scooping under the ball near the cloth. The proper way to jump a cue ball is by striking downward onto the top of it. One way is to hold the cue like a dart, with your back elbow upward at least 45 degrees and execute the shot with a quick pop and a motion similar to that of throwing a dart.

Some players prefer using phenolic tips for jumping because they are harder. Not only will repeatedly using a

### Jump over Blocker

- Line up your cue ball and an object ball in a straight line with a blocker ball in between.

- Elevate the butt of your cue 45 degrees. Choke up your grip by placing your back hand closer to your body.

- Execute the shot with a quick downward pop.

- Keep practicing! It is not easy to perform this jump shot consistently unless you are an advanced player.

### Slight Jump

- Set up two object balls next to each other with just less than one cue ball distance apart.

- Set up another object ball on the opposite side from where the cue ball is.

- You cannot shoot between the balls with a level cue, so you have to elevate slightly to hit your object ball.

- Elevate about 10 degrees and use a short, quick jab to jump the cue ball over the blockers.

normal tip cause the tip to mushroom, but also a normal tip will not cause as much of a rebound as a harder tip. If you do use a normal tip, make sure it is a hard one. Many players use the same cue they break with to jump with. Doing this also prolongs the life of the tip of their playing cue.

These jumping exercises will demonstrate shots that are possible with a normal cue. The number one thing to keep in the back of your mind as you attempt a jump shot is to have a loose grip with your backhand. If you are holding the cue stick too tight, you will not be able to get much jump.

## Jump off the Rail

- Your opponent left you with this safety shot.

- To make the hit and pocket your ball, you need to jump your cue ball off the rail and over your opponent's blocker ball.

- Elevate your cue at least 50 degrees and bridge over the object ball.

- Aim the cue ball directly at the rail, hit down on it with a short, fast jab, and bounce it off the cushion.

## Jump Bank

- This jump bank is a fairly easy one because the cue ball is only a few inches from the rail.

- This distance makes it easier to strike the cue ball. A good player will make this shot more often than not.

- Elevate the butt of your cue and shoot the cue ball directly into the rail.

- The cue ball will jump off the rail and bank back to sink your object ball in front of the pocket.

189

# DEFENSE PRACTICE

Beat the competition; practice defense and improve a skill that will help you win more games

A lot of players do not use nearly enough defenses. Gain a leg up on them when you practice your safety play skills. Learning to think smarter and execute good safety shots will help you get control of the table.

When you play safe, try to control only one ball—either the cue ball or the object ball— instead of both of them. Focus

on which ball is more important to control. Doing this will guide you in choosing a better safety shot. You will also come across some situations when you want to control both balls. Remember to identify these situations.

It is ideal to hide the object ball from the cue ball; however, doing this can take exceptional speed control. At times you

*Soft Touch*

- Many safeties require a soft touch on the cue ball.

- Set up a cluster of balls and begin by hitting just below center on the cue ball.

- The idea is to hit just enough to get the cue ball to the rail and land just behind another ball. The

target object ball should move slightly forward.

- This exercise helps you get a feel for using a light touch at only slightly moving balls.

*Stop Shot to Opposite Ends*

- Set up a couple of object balls next to each other and put the cue ball directly behind the rear one.

- Shoot into the rear object ball. Execute a stop shot so the cue lands behind the front object ball.

- The object ball you shot into will go to the opposite end of the table.

- Your opponent will be left hidden and with a long shot to kick at.

may not be able to hide the ball. Remember to assess your opponents' weaknesses and think of a defensive play that will leave them with a more difficult shot. Safety play involves a bit of creativity. Use yours to recognize more opportunities for playing defense.

Pay special attention to defense in practice. Notice how much of the object ball you need to hit to get the cue ball where you need to. You will be able to hook your opponent more often after you learn the path and speed control of the balls.

Practice defense to give you an advantage over others. Many players overlook defensive play in their practice and will try to make their shots more often than they will practice a safe. When you practice safeties, you gain the skills needed to overcome those players in a match. The main key to good defense is identifying contact points and the speed you need to use to send the balls along the correct path.

## Control the Cue Ball

- Send the cue ball behind blocking balls and the object ball away.

- Set up a cluster of balls near the corner pocket. Put an object ball near the rail and the cue ball about five diamonds down the table from it.

- Use below center on the cue ball and a one-quarter object ball hit.

- Repeat until you get the cue ball to land behind the blocker balls so there is no clear shot.

## Control the Object Ball

- Set up an object ball near the rail with the cue ball diagonally about two diamonds away.

- Shoot with low opposite English on the cue ball.

- The object ball will go up table to the center of the short rail, and the cue ball will come to the center of the short rail near you.

- Practice this shot, and you will soon develop a feel for controlling the object ball.

191

# STROKE DRILLS
## What you do off the table can help you on the table

Developing a fluid motion and follow-through is essential to having a good stroke. In preparation for the game, you can use objects other than the balls and use off-table exercises to develop a good stroke.

Pretend you are playing baseball and need to throw the baseball to your teammate on base. You can work with a partner or by yourself. Have a partner stand across the room from you. Throw a pillow underhanded toward him. Have

him catch it and throw it back toward you. When you practice alone, set up a waste basket to throw a crumpled ball of paper underhanded into it. Most importantly, your motion should be continuous, and you should concentrate on your follow-through.

When doing these drills, you get a feel for the motion of your arm and body and easily can apply it in your game play. Perform stretches to loosen up. Being tense when you

## Stretches to Loosen Up

• Benefit from practicing good stretching techniques and allow yourself to reduce tension.

• Sit on the floor, stretch out your arms, and bend forward to touch your toes.

• Raise your arms parallel to the floor and swing your arms side to side, turning at your torso.

• Roll your neck in circular motions.

• Put your arms out at your side and swing them in small forward circular motions. Continue with larger circular motions. Then reverse the circular motions.

### Plastic Bottle Drill

• Test your stroke for straightness by using a plastic bottle with a narrow neck.

• Set up the bottle on the table in front of you and stroke your cue into the neck of the bottle.

• Keep doing this until you stroke into it without hitting the sides.

• Try this with your eyes closed. Motion will become effortless so you can concentrate on the other aspects of your game.

play can affect your game. Breathing exercises can help you breathe regularly during a match and maintain focus and concentration.

Filling your mind with positive thoughts and reflecting on your successes will enable you to open your mind to learning more about the game. Negative thoughts will inhibit you from absorbing new information and may stunt your game play. When you hang on the shots you missed or on your scratches, you will most likely be unable to improve your game much further. Your mental game is just as important to apply in competition as are the physical skills you have learned thus far.

## Paper-in-basket Drill

- This is a good way to train on your follow-through.

- Crumple a piece of paper into a ball. Set up a waste basket across the room from you.

- Throw the paper underhanded into the waste basket. Do not expect to make the paper into the basket every time.

- More importantly, make sure that you have a fluid motion and that you are following through on your throw.

### Building Confidence

- When you practice to the point that a skill becomes automatic, your confidence level will rise to the occasion.

- Don't overthink your shots too much.

- Relax and have fun.

- Play naturally and effortlessly, allowing your body to take over your mind.

- Fill your mind with positive thoughts. Move forward, don't dwell on your misses; instead, recognize your accomplishments.

193

# FUN FOR EVERYONE
## Pool is a great game to enjoy with family and friends of all ages

In the past twenty years pool has become more and more a family game that is enjoyed by people of all ages. It doesn't matter if you are four years old and just learning the game or eighty-five years old and have been playing all your life. It is a game that remains fun and entertaining.

There is no better way to get together with friends and family and have a good time. Pool is one of the few sports in which age is not a major factor. You don't have to worry about injuries, and everyone can play. Many families and friends get together on a regular basis to play pool.

More and more upscale pool rooms are being built and are a great place for family and friends to go. They have restaurants and video games along with many other family activities. Many of these rooms are used to host birthday parties. The days of the smoke-filled pool rooms with no ventilation have long passed. But it is an unfair reputation that

### Family Fun

- Pool is a great way for family members to get together and enjoy themselves.

- What better way to enjoy time with your children than to teach them the game of pool?

- No matter what the age, everyone has fun. Pool can be played by children as young as four years old.

- The game has become more accessible as more families have brought pool tables into their homes.

### Young Children

- Guide the cue stick for children, especially when they have not yet learned the basics, to help give them more confidence.

- Here a father is helping his daughter line up a shot.

- The other child is able to watch and learn.

- The child is using the shorter, lighter cue for more control.

sometimes still haunts the billiard industry. If there is a pool room in your area, check it out. It is a great place to meet new friends. If the room has leagues, join a team. Remember that the more you play, the better you will get.

## GREEN ● LIGHT

Playing pool with family members is a great way to enjoy quality time. Learning pool at a young age will help a child acquire good hand-eye coordination. Pool is a game that everyone can enjoy, no matter what age. For seniors it is an inexpensive sport that can be enjoyed with others or even alone. It also is good exercise, both mentally and physically.

### Child with Mom

- Here a mother is playing a game of pool with her daughter.

- The popularity of pool among females is at an all-time high, particularly as more female professionals get the spotlight in televised events.

- Family time with Mom playing pool with her children is a great way to spend an afternoon or evening.

- The more the children see their parents play, the more interested the children will be in learning.

### Senior Play

- Pool is a game that everyone can play at any age.

- Many senior centers have pool tables.

- Pool is one of the most popular games for seniors. Many senior players shoot well, even into their eighties.

- Both relaxing and mentally stimulating, pool is a good game for those who want to keep up on their skills.

195

# EXHIBITIONS

## Nothing excites a crowd as much as a trick shot artist showing his stuff

Anyone who wants to be fascinated by the game of pool needs to attend a professional trick shot exhibition. Professional trick shot exhibitions are enjoyable to watch by players and nonplayers alike. Exhibitions are all about the audience having fun and being entertained.

Trick shot artists are the Harlem Globetrotters of pool,

especially the greatest of the great, Mike Massey, who has traveled over 3 million miles and performed in over forty-four countries.

This aspect of the sport is all about putting smiles on the faces of everyone in the audience. The popularity of exhibitions has risen because of the exposure the trick shot artists

### Boy Scouts

- Everyone enjoys a fun time, and the Boy Scouts of America are no exception.

- Doing trick shot exhibitions for youth groups such as the Boy Scouts is especially fun. Nothing is better than putting a smile on a child's face.

- An exhibition often opens children's eyes to the sport and gets them hooked on pool at a young age.

- Hosting exhibitions is a great way to reach out to children, let them have a little fun, and maybe get them to learn a thing or two about pool.

### Professionals and Amateurs

- The current number one trick shot artist in the world, Andy Segal, shows his unique form to his young audience.

- Children love to see trick shots. Such shots are sure to keep their attention.

- Trick shots artists such as Andy Segal know how to make an audience smile.

- If you want a great form of entertainment for your group, consider hiring a trick shot artist.

get on television. Corporations book more trick shot artists than ever before to draw large crowds.

Not only are large corporations booking shows, but also organizations such as the Boy Scouts and senior centers love to have on-location exhibitions for their patrons.

Exhibitions usually run for two to three hours beginning with a question and answer period, then a display of various trick shots. Then audience members get to play one game matches with the professional. When the challenge matches finish up, there is an autograph session.

There are only a few trick shot artists and professional pool players that are out there making a living off of exhibitions. There are many players who will do a handful of exhibitions each year. Doing exhibitions involves traveling from city to city. Mike Massey, Tom Rossman, and a few others are almost always on the road. Rarely do they spend more than a couple of days in any one city.

## Trick Shots for Seniors

- Audiences of all ages enjoy watching trick shots. Senior centers are popular venues for trick shot exhibitions, and such displays liven up the day of seniors.

- Seniors enjoy the entertainment that a trick shot exhibition brings.

- Other organizations, such as the Knights of Columbus and the Elks Club, also host exhibitions for their members.

- Check out local organizations for a trick shot show in your area.

## Finger Pool

- This special exhibition trick by Mike Massey is called "finger pool."

- He takes the cue ball with one hand and rolls it down the table with an unbelievable amount of spin on it.

- He can make the cue ball go the length of the table and spin straight across without touching the rail.

- If you have the chance, see an exhibition featuring Mike Massey.

197

# UNDER TEN YEARS OLD
## A child can stand on a box if he or she can't reach the table

What better way to connect to your son or daughter than to teach him or her how to play pool? It is a game that anyone can play, no matter what age. Making it a fun time will keep your child's interest in the game for many years to come. Many families get together to play pool throughout their lifetimes.

For children under the age of ten, progress will come a little bit more slowly than with older children. But teaching children

the basics of pool at this age will help them develop good habits that they'll carry with them throughout their lives. Be sure that you always use words of encouragement because a child is more likely to become frustrated and turned off from the sport if too much negative feedback is given.

One of the biggest challenges is keeping a child's attention. It is important that you make each experience enjoyable. Do not try to force the game on children. If they see that you are

### Learning the Basics

- Learning is always more fun when you have your friends or siblings with you.

- Here the three girls take instruction on how to place their hand on the table and make a bridge.

- They are having fun while learning the basics.

- Learning the correct way at a young age will help to eliminate bad habits later on.

### Shorter, Lighter Cues

- It is important that the equipment fits the person.

- Younger children need to use a shorter, lighter cue.

- The average cue is 58 inches long and weighs 19 ounces. This is too long and heavy for young children.

- They will find controlling the cue difficult.

- You can find the right-size cue at your local dealer.

having fun, they will naturally want to join in.

When starting out, teach children only one or two skills each time up at the table. If you try to show children too much, they will become discouraged and lose interest. The more time they stay on the table and play, the more they will want to learn.

For children under ten, it is a good idea to have an adult around. They need to learn about caring for the table and the cue sticks, and they may need a little help actually reaching the table to shoot.

## Milk Crate Pool

- A box comes in handy for the younger players. Young children may not be tall enough to reach the table.

- With a box to stand on, they will enjoy the game much more.

- The box will also allow them to address the shot in the correct position.

- Some families build a stand that goes completely around the table so that their younger children can shoot from anywhere.

## Coaching Children

- Just as when teaching in other sports, you must be patient when teaching a child to play pool.

- Pushing a child too much will only discourage him from wanting to play more.

- Without positive reinforcements, your child will be easily discouraged and quickly lose interest in the game.

- You need to be with your child when he is first starting so you can teach him how to respect the equipment because it is easy to damage.

199

# JUNIOR LEAGUE & PLAYERS

## Playing in a junior league will help you prepare your game at a younger age

Most young players start playing pool at home or at a friend's house. Others learn at the local boys' or girls' club or social center. But a trend nowadays is to have younger players shoot in junior leagues.

Junior leagues are becoming more popular throughout the United States and even worldwide. With almost every pool room being nonsmoking, younger players have become regulars. There is no better way for young players to learn the game than by joining a league. They learn the rules of pool and also learn how to interact with other people around a pool table. They also learn different games and variations.

In junior leagues it is a good idea to have an adult on each

### *Junior League*

- Starting off as a junior and playing in leagues will help to develop your game at a young age.

- You learn the correct rules and etiquette of league play.

- League play teaches teenagers how to socialize and make new friends.

- League play develops good sportsmanship.

### *Teaching Responsibilities*

- Playing on a team helps teenagers learn responsibility.

- Children play to win not only for themselves but also for every member of their team.

- Being captain of a team helps them learn how to make decisions.

- Junior teams should give everyone a chance at being captain. It is a valuable learning opportunity.

team or at least an adult present to help supervise. Depending on the age group of the league, you need to keep young players focused on the match. Shorter matches help with that.

Junior leagues should never award money at the end of the league year. Prizes are much better. Young players remember trophies and prizes much longer than money.

The best way to organize a junior league is to have your children gather a bunch of their friends. Leagues for juniors are usually held on Saturday mornings. It is best to limit teams to three players. As mentioned, keeping their interest is important. It is a good idea to have an adult available to help juniors with their game. If your league has an instructor, make a table available where junior players can ask questions and get some pool lessons.

## Fun With Friends

- League play helps develop social skills for younger players.

- Being on a team will help make it easy to find new friends who share a common interest in the game of pool.

- League play will also condition young players to compete for competitions and playing in tournaments.

- Being a captain will help with decision making and learning about responsibility.

### Tips from the Pros

- Receive instruction from an experienced player who understands the fundamentals of the game.

- Learn how to pocket balls first and then move on to cue ball control.

- The practice drills in this book will help you to become a better player.

- Concentrate during your practice sessions as much as you would during a tournament.

# ENTERTAINING YOUR GUESTS

## Your audience will be amazed at the trick shots you will be able to perform

To keep an audience's attention, you need to make eye contact—not with just the first row of people but with everyone in the room. Make sure that you can be heard. Take your time and never rush a trick shot. Explain the shot in detail and then take your time and make the shot. If you find yourself missing a couple of shots in a row, choose an easy shot that you know you can make. The enthusiasm of the crowd will drain quickly if you keep missing shots.

At every party you always have a heckler. The best way to handle a heckler is to have him make a shot. You will win him over, and he will become your best audience member.

Always open with your favorite easy trick shot. You want

### Just Showing Off

- When practicing for a show, be aware of how much time you need for the number of shots you shoot.

- You need to create a good flow to your exhibition.

- It is far better to have ten shots that you can make consistently than twenty shots that you make only half the time.

- Always keep your audience entertained even when you are just setting up your shots.

### Know Your Lines

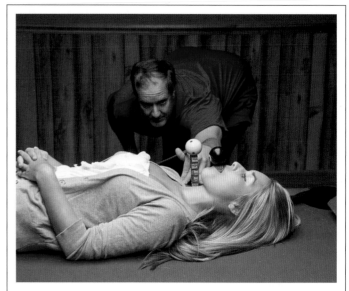

- To be a good entertainer, you need to have a story to go along with each trick shot.

- Have an entertaining line ready for when you miss a shot.

- If you miss a couple of shots in a row, make sure to follow up with an easy shot.

- Having a funny line when you miss a shot can be just as entertaining as making a shot.

to start your show on a positive note. If you start off with jump shots, begin with an easy one and work your way up to more-difficult ones. The same applies to massé shots.

Props are great to add into your show. Props decorate an easy shot and make it look spectacular. You always want to keep the audience's attention. Sometimes throwing in a joke or a couple of good one-liners will help, especially after you have missed a couple of shots.

Always be confident. Speak loudly and make that eye contact. You can pick someone from the audience to shoot one of your setup shots. Everyone enjoys seeing his or her buddy going to the table to shoot a trick shot. Above all, have fun!

## Get the Audience Involved

- You need to have a couple of setup shots that a person from the audience will be able to perform.

- Your audience members will love it and will be thrilled when they make the shots.

- Remember that the more difficult the shot, the better the person from the audience needs to be.

- Set up numerous shots with different degrees of difficulty so that you can get people of different playing abilities involved.

## Tap in Shots

- For setup shots you can lightly tap the top of the ball into position. You need to do this before everyone arrives.

- Doing this allows you to check out the shot and make any necessary adjustments.

- Tapping the balls into place saves time when setting up the shots during the show.

- Tapping the balls lightly keeps them frozen together and in place. Tapping does not hurt the table as long as you do it lightly.

203

# ALLISON FISHER

## "The Duchess of Doom" from England started playing Snooker at a very young age

Allison Fisher has been making a name for herself ever since she picked up her first cue stick at age seven. Born and raised in England, she played Snooker, field hockey, basketball, netball, and javelin. At only age fourteen, Allison committed to just one sport and become a professional Snooker player. She won her first National event at fifteen and first World Championship at seventeen. Within ten years, Allison won eleven World titles: seven individual and four doubles partnering Steve Davis.

Allison moved to the United States in September 1995 at age twenty-seven and became a WPBA professional pool player. Ranked number one by September 1996, she held this position for eleven of the next twelve years. Allison has been

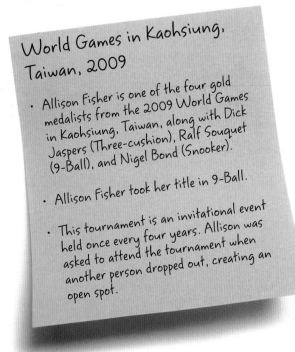

**World Games in Kaohsiung, Taiwan, 2009**

- Allison Fisher is one of the four gold medalists from the 2009 World Games in Kaohsiung, Taiwan, along with Dick Jaspers (Three-cushion), Ralf Souquet (9-Ball), and Nigel Bond (Snooker).

- Allison Fisher took her title in 9-Ball.

- This tournament is an invitational event held once every four years. Allison was asked to attend the tournament when another person dropped out, creating an open spot.

*BCA Hall of Fame Inductees, 2009*

- Allison Fisher and Johnny Archer in October 2009 when they were both inducted into the BCA Hall of Fame.

- Allison and Johnny were both inducted into the Greatest Player category reserved for outstanding players who are active in

competition for at least twenty years and have won at least one championship.

- This is an important recognition in the sport that not many players receive.

- Johnny and Allison were voted players of the decade in the Billiards Press.

the spokesperson for many industry companies, including Cuetec Cues, Kasson Tables, American Pool Players Association, Championship Cloth, and Delta-13 Racks. Allison contributes to numerous charities, including St. Jude Children's Research. She also offers assistance with private fundraisers. Allison has been regularly featured on ESPN and international television. She has achieved over seventy-five professional titles, including fifty-three WPBA Classic tour titles and twenty-two other international titles.

Allison holds the record for most consecutive wins on the WPBA Classic Tour totaling seven. She also holds the most wins with eight U.S. National 9-Ball Championships, five Tournament of Champions, four U.S. Open Championships, and four WPA World 9-Ball Championships. Allison was voted Player of the Decade and Player of the Year for eleven of the twelve years since 1996. In 2009, she won a Gold Medal in the World Games representing Great Britain. Later that year, she was inducted into the BCA Hall of Fame.

## *Korea versus World Team Championship, 2009*

- This photo is of Allison Fisher competing in the Third Annual Korea versus World Team Championship, held in May 2009.

- This is an outdoor event at the La Festa Shopping Mall in Bucheon, Korea.

- Some of the brightest stars of billiards today participate.

- The World Team consisted of Captain George Breedlove (USA), Allison Fisher (ENG), Shanelle Loraine (GUAM), and newbie Zarah Delrosario (PHL). Team Korea featured Captain Hyun Ho Kim, Yu Ram Cha, Gui Young Lee, and Jeanette Lee.

## *Brighton Walk of Fame, Great Britain*

- Allison Fisher was honored as a celebrity on the Brighton walk of fame.

- Brighton is the first official walk next to Hollywood made specifically for the United Kingdom and the rest of Europe.

- There are plaques with the names of a variety of celebrities, such as authors, musicians, entertainers, heroes, and sports persons.

- The arrival of the Brighton Walk was celebrated by over thirty-five celebrities and hundreds of guests on November 3, 2002.

# GERDA HOFSTATTER

## "G Force," an Austrian-born billiard lover turned pro, is one of the perennial stars of the WPBA

In her youth, Gerda competed in tennis, skiing, and fencing. She won the Austrian and International Junior Fencing Championships before deciding to focus exclusively on pool.

Gerda joined a local billiard team in her Austrian hometown. Inspired at age sixteen by the beauty of the sport, her love for the game took hold. Gerda entered individual

tournaments and quickly became the Austrian National Champion. A few years later, she earned Austria's first Gold Medal in the European Championships. In recognition of her accomplishments, Gerda's hometown awarded her an honorary gold medal and a key to the city.

In 1990, Gerda moved to Sweden to study and compete in

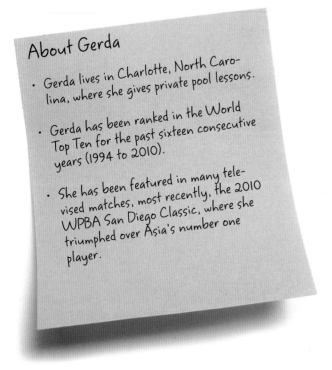

### About Gerda

- Gerda lives in Charlotte, North Carolina, where she gives private pool lessons.

- Gerda has been ranked in the World Top Ten for the past sixteen consecutive years (1994 to 2010).

- She has been featured in many televised matches, most recently, the 2010 WPBA San Diego Classic, where she triumphed over Asia's number one player.

*WPBA San Diego Classic, 2010*

- The San Diego Classic was held at the Viejas Casino in Alpine, California.

- Gerda defeated Monica Webb, Ga-Young Kim, and Karen Corr in single elimination rounds as she neared the finals.

- In the finals, Hofstatter bested China's Chang, who defeated major players on her way to the final face-off with Gerda.

- It was Gerda's first tournament win on the Classic Tour since her BCA Open win of 2000. Gerda considers this her favorite victory.

the sport. Then, after garnering Europe's top player ranking for two consecutive years, Gerda moved to the United States in 1993 and joined the Women's Professional Billiard Association (WPBA). Gerda won her first event and remains the only person to have done so in WPBA history.

Gerda's wins include a WPA World 9-Ball Championship in 1995, a U.S. National WPBA 9-Ball Championship in 1997, a BCA Open 9-Ball Championship in 2000, eleven European Championships, seventeen Austrian National Championships, and nine WPBA Classic Tour Championships.

Gerda is sponsored by Predator Cues and she endorses the CueTrack stroke-training aid. She supports multiple charitable causes, particularly Susan G. Komen for the Cure and Make-A-Wish Foundation.

## *WPBA U.S. Open 9-Ball Championship, 2009*

- The U.S. Open 9-Ball Championship is an annual event since 1976.

- The women's division requires qualification based on points earned through the WPBA tour.

- The women play in Norman, Oklahoma, at the Riverwind Casino. Gerda made it to the television rounds and was bested by the eventual champion, Korean Ga-Young Kim, in the semi-finals.

- The U.S. Open Championship is one title that Gerda hasn't won yet and remains one of her dreams as an athlete.

### Gerda Outside of Pool

- Gerda has many other interests outside of pool. One of them is piloting glider planes.

- These aircrafts use air currents, called thermals, to glide through the air without power.

- Gliders can soar through the air for hours by using lift (vertical air movement) to climb.

- Gerda's other interests include yoga, Tai Chi, golf, and reading.

# LARRY HUBBART

## "The Iceman" played on the professional tour and cofounded the American Poolplayers Association

Larry Hubbart was born and raised in Rochester, New York, and has played pool since the age of fourteen. He played on the professional tour for many years and has seventeen open tournament wins in 8-Ball and 9-Ball and seven 14.1 wins. Larry earned five titles in the Western and Central New York Championships in addition to two New York open titles.

Larry's other achievements include titles in the 1975 National 9-Ball Championship, 1976 Eastern Open 9-Ball Championship, 1977 World 8-Ball Championship (defeating Jersey Red), 1977 World 9-Ball Championship (defeating Wade Crane), 1979 Tournament of Champions in Albuquerque, New Mexico, and 1979 World 9-Ball Championship in

### Vice President of PBA

- Larry Hubbart served as Vice President for the Professional Billiards Association (PBA).

- The PBA is comprised of male professional players in America.

- The board was created to improve the lives of professional players, acting as a central information center.

- The PBA established official 9-Ball rules in 1985 that were inaugurated in a Classic Cup event and printed in the *Pool and Billiards Almanac*.

### Larry Hubbart Tournament Play

- Larry had a great year in 1983 when he took the title in the Texas River City Open.

- That same year, Larry took second place in the Music City Open 9-Ball Tournament. This is an annual tournament and was held in Nashville, Tennessee.

- In 1984, Larry took fifth place in an Austin tournament and seventh place in a U.S. Open.

- In the fourth annual Classic Cup, held in Chicago, Larry tied with Buddy Hall for third place.

Baltimore, Maryland. His playing abilities during the 1960s and 70s were equal to or better than most top professional players of that era.

Larry's major accomplishments have been in 1975 when he bested Steve Mizerak in the finals of the National 9-Ball Championship in 1978 when he took the title in the Tournament of Champions and in 1979 when he defeated Larry Liscotti in the finals of the World 9-Ball Championship.

Larry marketed a line of cues, which was put in production by Meucci. These cues are a rare find and collector's items.

Larry Hubbart co-founded the National Pool League with fellow professional Terry "Texas Terry" Bell, who developed the idea when he realized how popular billiards was becoming. Terry Bell and Larry joined together in 1979 to form this league, which then became the American Poolplayers Association (APA) in 1981. The APA is the word's largest organized league system and has expanded outside of the United States to both Canada and Japan (known as the CPA in Canada and JPA in Japan).

## American Poolplayers Association Cofounder

## National Team Championships

- Larry Hubbart and Terry Bell were strong business partners and founders of the APA.

- Terry came up with the idea when he realized the growing popularity of billiards.

- Terry and Larry joined forces and together they created and developed a handicap system based on their knowledge of pool.

- In 1979, the league was first named the National Pool League. Previous names for the league include the American Pool League, the Busch Pool League, and the Bud Light Pool League.

- Larry (shown with his wife above) wore many hats. Not only did he play professional pool, serving as Vice President of the PBA and cofounder of the APA, but he also performed trick shot ex hibitions.

- Larry opened the 1985 Busch Pool League $35,000 National Tournament with an exhibition.

- The league holds national tournaments in Las Vegas twice annually, once for singles and doubles championships and the second time for team tournaments. Competitions are held in 8-Ball and 9-Ball formats.

# EWA MATAYA LAURANCE
## "The Striking Viking" from Sweden fell in love with pool as a teenager and dove right into the billiard profession

Ewa instantly fell in love with pool at age fourteen when she went to a billiard room with her brother near their hometown in Sweden. Captivated by the game, she practiced six to ten hours a day. That same year she entered a major tournament and finished in fourth place. The following year, Ewa took her first title in a Swedish 9-Ball tournament.

Two years later, Ewa entered a Swedish 14.1 championship and won, qualifying her for the European Championship. Ewa then won the European Championship in Switzerland; as a result, she was invited to the World Championship held in New York City. Ewa was only seventeen.

Ewa's trip to the United States marked an entry into her

### International Trick Shot Challenge, 2005

- Ewa Mataya Laurance is one of four women who qualified to compete in the 2005 International Trick Shot Challenge held in Las Vegas.

- Ewa joined in competition with Allison Fisher, Gerda Hofstatter, and Dawn Hopkins.

- Ewa, top ranked WPBA pro and BCA Hall of Famer, bested Allison Fisher in the finals, giving her a victorious first place finish.

- Winning this event marked Ewa's first pro title since the 1998 Brunswick Boston Classic.

### World Cup of Trick Shots, 2007

- The 2007 *World Cup of Trick Shots* was held at Mohegan Sun in Connecticut.

- Team Europe was composed of trick shot champions captain Stefano Pelinga, Ewa Laurance, Nick Nikolaidis, and Luke Szywala.

- Team USA included trick shot champions captain Mike Massey, Jeanette Lee, Tom Rossman, and Bruce Barthelette (2006 Masters Artistic Pool runner-up).

- Team Europe competed against Team USA in eight artistic shots and won, claiming the Gold Medal.

professional pool career, as she decided to stay. Since becoming a WPBA professional in 1981, Ewa earned many titles, including two U.S. Open 9-Ball Championships, two World Open 9-Ball Championships, three Swedish 9-Ball Championships, two player of the year awards, high run world record holder in women's competitive Straight Pool, WPBA sportsperson of the year, Billiard and Bowling Institute of America award, and four WPBA Classic Tour titles (the tour which Ewa helped launch).

## Generationpool.com 9-Ball Championship

- In this photo, Ewa Mataya Laurance is lining up a shot at the 2005 Generationpool .com 9-Ball Championship held in Las Vegas.

- This event attracted the top professional players from around the world in both the men's and women's division.

- The women's division began with sixty-four players with the final two matches featured on television.

- Ewa placed third after being defeated by Karen Corr in the semi-finals.

## Ewa's Interests

- When Ewa is not playing pool, you can often find her on the golf course.

- She enjoys traveling, reading, photography, and gardening.

- Ewa is also an animal lover. She lives in South Carolina with her family and her dogs, cats, and horses.

- In July 2009, Ewa became an APA League Operator with her husband Mitch, an ESPN commentator who also promotes the league there.

# MIKE MASSEY

## "The Tennessee Tarzan" is an American professional billiard player, trick shot artist, and pool instructor

Mike Massey was born in 1947 and took up pool as a teenager. He played pool for fifty years prior to 2010 and is a world renowned trick shot artist since the late seventies. Mike earned his nickname "The Tennessee Tarzan" early on when he used to wear long hair, hustle pool, and arm wrestle. Mike is a pool instructor and travels around the world to perform exhibitions and give lessons. Mike met his wife, Francine, twenty-two years ago when she took a lesson from him.

Mike's first professional title was won in a 1971 National 9-Ball Championship. Since then he has won titles in the 1982 National 9-Ball Championship, 1996 Dutch National 8-Ball Championship, and 1996 Hall of Fame 8-Ball

### BCA Hall of Fame, 2005

- Mike Massey was inducted into the BCA Hall of Fame Meritorious Service category.

- Meritorious Service is awarded to individuals who have made lasting impressions and major contributions to the billiard profession.

- Mike Massey has been considered pool's best trick shot artist by many for at least thirty years and performs exhibitions globally.

- Mike also assisted with many TV movies, books, and billiard publications

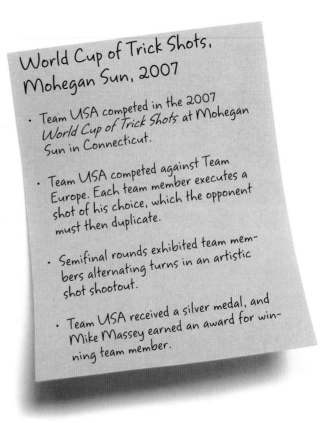

### World Cup of Trick Shots, Mohegan Sun, 2007

- Team USA competed in the 2007 World Cup of Trick Shots at Mohegan Sun in Connecticut.

- Team USA competed against Team Europe. Each team member executes a shot of his choice, which the opponent must then duplicate.

- Semifinal rounds exhibited team members alternating turns in an artistic shot shootout.

- Team USA received a silver medal, and Mike Massey earned an award for winning team member.

Championship. He was the 1996 Mosconi Cup winning team member for Team USA and won the 1997 Senior Masters 9-Ball Championship.

Well known for trick shots, Mike is a two-time National BCA Trick Shot Champion. He won seventeen major trick shot championships, including five *Trick Shot Magic*, four WPA World Artistic (which he also took second place in three times), three World Snooker Trick Shots in England, and one Legends of Trick Shots in Ukraine.

Mike was inducted into the BCA Hall of Fame in 2005, and he holds records for high runs of nine in tournament play and thirteen in challenge match play. Mike also has a high run in Straight Pool of 224 balls. In twenty-four-hour marathons, Mike ran 11,230 balls, 8,030 balls one-handed, and 330 racks of 9-Ball in Austria on live television (not including early 9 ball combinations or making the 9 on the break).

Mike has been involved in several television appearances, his biggest being in "The Baron and The Kid" with Johnny Cash. Mike also wrote a book with Phil Capelle called *Mike Massey's World of Trick Shots*.

## Mike Massey and Finger Pool

- Mike Massey is noted for his finger pool talents.

- This is a memorable showing where Mike takes a ball in his hand.

- He spins the ball out of his hand and throws it down table with a tremendous amount of English.

- In doing this, the ball curves behind a blocker ball, hugs the rail and pockets another ball in the corner.

## Fun Facts: Mike Massey

- Mike has traveled to over twenty-five countries as well as the entire United States to perform trick shot exhibitions.

- Mike has appeared in seven movies and has greatly contributed to others, including the Minnesota Fats trick shot video, for which Mike set up shots.

- Mike has been given the title of Greatest Trick Shot artist ever by his peers.

- Mike was voted "Best in the History of the Game" by major billiard publications.

# ANDY SEGAL

"The Magic Man" is a well-known artistic pool champion, currently sitting at the top of the rankings for his talent

Andy Segal started competing in trick shot competitions back in 2002. His first tournament was the North American Championship, where he finished in fourth place. A few months later he finished fifth in the World Artistic Pool Championships in Kiev, Ukraine. It was all upward path from there. As luck would have it, he got a last-minute invite to the

2003 ESPN *Trick Shot Magic* six days before the event. Andy went on to finish second at the event and has been invited to every televised trick shot event since. His first major win was at the 2004 North Eastern Open, quickly followed a couple of months later by the 2004 Las Vegas Open. Overall, Andy has won over fifteen major trick shot titles. In 2009, he won

*Las Vegas Open, 2004*

- This photo was taken at the 2004 Las Vegas Open, held at the Riviera Hotel and Casino during the APA National Team Championships.

- Andy Segal is seen with his wife, Kimberly, in this photo, both holding the championship trophy

immediately following the final match.

- Around Andy's neck are three discipline (category) medals for having the highest individual score in the Prop/Novelty, Draw, and Massé disciplines.

*World Cup, 2008*

- This photo shows Andy Segal with partners Bruce Barthelette, Mike Massey and Tom Rossman at the 2008 ESPN *World Cup of Trick Shots* at Mohegan Sun Casino in Uncasville, Connecticut.

- They were partnered

together against the European team.

- Team USA, captained by Andy Segal was victorious.

- In the four years that the event has been held, Team USA has won three times and Team Europe once.

five out of the six championships, narrowly missing at the third annual Dr. Cue Artistic Cup in Maryland. Some of his titles include being a three-time Masters champion, three-time Ultimate Trick Shot champion, two-time Comet Classic Champion, World Artistic Pool Champion, three-time ESPN *World Cup of Trick Shots* Champion, and ESPN *Trick Shot Magic* Champion.

Andy has also worked in the television and film industry. He made an appearance in commercials for AT&T, All Detergent, and LiquidWick Pool Cues. He worked as a game show host in a pilot filmed for a major talent agency, and was a technical advisor in a Woody Allen film called *Sweet & Lowdown*, starring Woody Allen, Sean Penn, and Uma Thurman.

Andy is currently an APA League Operator in Hudson County, New Jersey. He is married to Kimberly Segal and has one daughter named Jessica. He is currently working to achieve his black belt in mixed martial arts.

## *World Trick Shot Championship, 2007*

- This photo was taken at The Lider Club in St. Petersburg, Russia, at the 2007 World Artistic Pool Championship.

- Andy Segal was warming up for his final match against Sebastian Giumelli from Argentina.

- The match came down to the final massé shot.

- Andy made it on his first attempt, tying up the match, and went on to win in a sudden death playoff.

## *Trick Shot Magic, 2009*

- Andy Segal won his first ESPN *Trick Shot Magic* in 2009 at New York New York Hotel and Casino in Las Vegas.

- His first match was a close one against Jamey Gray, the current world champion.

- The semi-final round was played against Nick Nikolaidis and was even closer.

- This long-awaited title finally came when Andy defeated Sebastian Giumelli, a rematch of the World Championships in Russia.

# LEAGUE PLAY

## Joining a pool league can help your game

Playing in a league is great for everyone because no matter what their age or gender, everyone can play. Younger players love the thrill of the competition. Older players love the competition and don't have to worry about getting injured.

When people play on a team, they create camaraderie among their fellow players. They are playing not just for themselves but for everyone on the team. This atmosphere helps them maintain focus and makes them better players.

When you form a team, you want to play with friends who get along and are out to have fun. You don't want a teammate who is a distraction. All it takes to ruin a good night is one player. So choose your teammates carefully. You can easily get teammates from the place you work or the place you most often play pool. It is a great night out of fun.

More leagues exist today than ever before. League play is a great way to make new friends. Another reason for the

### Organized Teams

- As in sports such as basketball, baseball, and football, many pool leagues are set up in teams.

- Each team has a captain who selects the remaining members of the team.

- Pool teams can have two members or more. Teams commonly have up to eight members.

- Players usually outnumber matches; therefore, some play and some sit out each week.

### Team Matches

- Matches between 2 players are usually played one at a time while the other team members watch. On league nights teams normally play five matches.

- Score sheets are used to keep track of innings, defenses, timeouts, wins, and losses.

- The winner of the lag is listed first. An inning is marked after the player listed second finishes shooting.

- Teams cannot give advice to their player during his turn unless he takes a timeout. For each timeout only one team member can coach.

popularity of teams is that local taverns and billiard rooms have a guaranteed crowd each week. As with bowling and darts, leagues are good for business. Also, teams are loyal to their host location, which means they go there on other nights to practice their game.

## League Tournaments

- In addition to weekly team play, many leagues have playoff tournaments.

- In playoffs teams hand their paperwork directly to the tournament director after the match is finished.

- Teams should tell the tournament director who won the match. The winning team advances to the next playoff round.

- The tournament director then gets the winning team's new paperwork ready for its next match. Teams pick up their paperwork for their next match time.

## National Tournaments

- Teams that advance through a series of playoff tournaments can win a spot in a national tournament.

- National team tournaments are usually held once a year in a designated city; many of them are held in Las Vegas.

- National tournaments are run like league playoffs. Winning teams hand in the match paperwork.

- The winning team captain is responsible for knowing the next scheduled match time and for getting his team there.

217

# HANDICAPS

## Just as in golf and bowling, all players in a pool league have a handicap

When you play in a pool league, from your first night of play onward, you are assigned a handicap. Depending on your skill, you either have to give up games or get spotted games. This process gives players of different abilities a fair chance to win.

Golf, bowling, pool, and many other sports use a handicapping system simply to give everyone a fair chance to compete and win against players of different abilities. If there were no handicaps, then only the best players would play in the league. The less-skilled players would have difficult time getting on a team.

Each pool league uses its own system for handicapping

### Strategies for Matching Players

- Teams want to match players in a way that will give them the best chance to win.

- Some teams match players with the same handicap, whereas others mismatch players.

- Know whether your players play better against the same skill level, a higher skill level, or a lower skill level and match appropriately.

- What is the match score? Is your team up or down? Use stronger players when you are down and consider using weaker players when you are up.

### Lagging

- The two players selected for the match often lag to determine who breaks.

- Both players go up to the table, shake hands, and wish each other good luck before they lag.

- Stroke the ball to the end rail and back. The ball that comes closest to the rail you stroke from wins the lag.

- When a ball hits the side rail or goes into a pocket, the other player wins the lag.

players. Generally, the higher the handicap number a player has, the more skilled the player. No matter what league you play in, the main thing is to have fun. If you are going out each week to play, you want your night to be enjoyable. Pool leagues have been around for the past thirty years or so and have seen significant growth.

Handicaps are calculated in different ways according to each league. For handicaps to work properly, players must keep accurate score. Because each team has its own score sheet, it gives the league operator two score sheets to look at.

## Handicapped Races

- A player's skill level determines how many games he needs in order to win a match. Some leagues base it on ball count.

- Look up races in a skill level race chart on the score sheet or in the rulebook.

- Each player races to his number of games or balls needed. The first player to reach his number wins the match.

- A skill level race is designed to give either player a fair chance to win.

## Tallying Wins and Losses

- Each game box on the score sheet has a spot to mark each game won.

- When the player listed first wins a game, the mark goes in the top of the box and vice versa.

- When the matches have been completed, each team totals up the number games won and lost for each player.

- The match point goes to the team whose player won.

# USING TIMEOUTS
## Proper use of timeouts is critical to winning or losing

When playing in a league, shooters are allowed to stop play and ask for advice. Doing this is called taking a "timeout." When and how timeouts are used is important.

Lower-skilled players are allowed two timeouts per game, and higher-skilled players are allowed one. Knowing when to use them is important.

If two lower-handicap players are playing, it is a good idea to save the timeouts for the end of the game. Too often captains waste a timeout when many balls are left on the table. Wait until near the end of the game when the timeout is needed more. You should call an early timeout only if the player is going to knock in the 8 ball.

If two higher-skilled players are shooting, the timeout may be called at any point in the game. Most higher-skilled players know what to do, but it never hurts to seek a second opinion.

### Hidden Cue Ball

- When a player cannot make a good hit, a timeout is a good idea.

- Coaches should know their players' strokes so they can tell them how to hit the cue ball.

- A coach can point to a spot on the rail for the player to aim at but must back away before the shot is taken.

- Most importantly, help make the hit so the opponent doesn't get ball-in-hand.

### Problem Balls

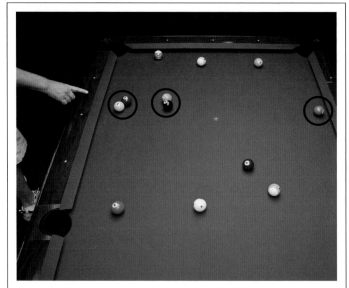

- A timeout may be necessary for problem balls (as circled).

- A coach should advise a player when or how to break the balls out or how to play a defense.

- Many lower-skilled players do not use defense shots as often as higher-skilled players do.

- A timeout can be used to educate a player on the alternatives he has in situations with problem balls.

Calling a timeout should only be done by the captain or the player. Timeouts should take no more than two minutes. In an effort to save time and confusion, only the coach can approach the table and talk to the player. The coach must walk away when the player is ready to shoot. Use your timeouts carefully. It can make the difference between winning and losing the game.

## Scratch Shot

- Timeouts are often used when a player or coach sees a scratch shot.

- A coach can help determine where or how to hit the ball to avoid a scratch.

- Even if you miss the shot, you are less likely to give your opponent ball-in-hand.

- The last thing you want to do is scratch on the 8 ball, especially when your opponent has all of his balls on the table.

## Avoiding an 8 Ball Foul

- You should use a timeout anytime during the rack if your player is about to knock in the 8 ball early.

- An 8 ball out of turn is an automatic loss of game. Avoid this shot at all costs.

- Coach your player to shoot a different shot or play safe.

- If no other clean shot is possible, try making a hit on something else. Even giving ball-in-hand is better than accidentally knocking in an 8 ball.

# THE TEAM CAPTAIN

A captain's responsibilities involve keeping score, sending in the score sheets, and knowing the rules

The most important position on the team is that of captain. The captain has the most responsibilities. But as captain, you also can pick which of your teammates you want to play each week. You also can match players for each set of games.

A captain needs to be a responsible person whom everyone on the team can trust and respect. He must be able to keep his team members informed of where the matches are each week and of who will play. On league night he is responsible for having someone keep score, whether that person is himself or someone else. When a problem or a question arises, the captain should be the player who resolves it.

Some players enjoy being captain, whereas others don't.

## Choosing a Player

- Before the first player is chosen, the home team flips a coin. The away team calls it in the air.

- Winner of the toss decides which team puts up first. Captains decide who plays each match.

- After a captain announces his player choice to the opposing team captain, he cannot change his mind.

- The other team captain then decides whom to match with that player.

## Signing Paperwork

- At the end of the night captains tally up the points and sign the paperwork.

- Signing paperwork indicates that you agree that the score is correct. Do not sign if you question the score.

- You should check the opposing team's paperwork to make sure both teams have the correct points tallied.

- Doing this saves you time and phone calls to the league office to make a correction.

Everyone is different, and sometimes a special person is needed to keep everyone happy. Captains need to make sure that everyone shows up at the matches and that everyone gets in enough scores.

At the end of the evening, the captain is responsible for collecting league dues from his players. He must check all paperwork from both his team and his opponents for accuracy. He then must either drop it off or put it in the mail so that the league office will receive it in time.

During playoffs the captain must notify his team members of where and when they will play. He must also let all the players read the weekly newsletter so they know what's happening in their league. The best captains are ones who lead by example. They are polite and respectful to their opponents and teammates. They are always on time with their paperwork and keep their team well informed.

## *Mailing Paperwork*

- A captain's responsibilities continue even after paperwork is signed and league night is over.

- The league office needs the original paperwork to give applicable bonus points and enter team scores.

- Many captains fax paperwork in before mailing. Include any applicable correspondence.

- Write a check, stamp the envelope, and mail it that night or the next morning.

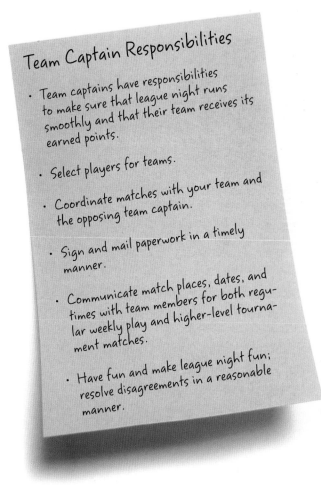

### Team Captain Responsibilities

- Team captains have responsibilities to make sure that league night runs smoothly and that their team receives its earned points.

- Select players for teams.

- Coordinate matches with your team and the opposing team captain.

- Sign and mail paperwork in a timely manner.

- Communicate match places, dates, and times with team members for both regular weekly play and higher-level tournament matches.

- Have fun and make league night fun; resolve disagreements in a reasonable manner.

# LEARNING THE RULES

## To be a good captain or player, you must know the rules; be sure to read the rule book

Every team receives a rule book. But as the old saying goes, you can lead a horse to water, but you can't make him drink. Too often players don't know the rules and end up costing their team a game. Each league has slightly different rules, but the majority of them are the same. Learn the rules!

There is no worse feeling than losing a game or a match because you didn't know the rules. Be sure to study all the rules ahead of time. Have all your players read the rule book also so that if the captain is unable to attend a match, someone else who knows the rules will be there. Knowledge is power. If you know the rules, and you see the other team breaking them, you can speak up.

### Rule Books

- Rule books are given to each captain. League rules can also be found online on the league Web sites. They contain a set of national rules used in all league areas.

- Rule books provide guidance so that league members know what to do in different situations.

- Knowing the rules and following them ensures that league play is fair for everyone.

- Have the rule book with you on league night in case you need to look up something.

### Bylaws

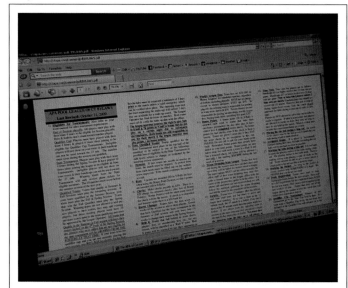

- Bylaws contain rules that may be different from one league area to the next.

- These are rules for your league area and may be based on feedback that the league operator received.

- These rules cannot be enforced when you play in another area or nationally.

- Bylaws are another tool you should have with you on league night to answer frequently asked questions.

Many leagues list their rules on their Web site. You can direct your players there, or you can make copies of the rule book to hand out to each player. Leagues may also have a section called "bylaws," which are rules that apply only to teams at the local level. Usually these bylaws are put in place to cover local ordinances. Be sure to read and understand each one. If you have any questions, call your local league office. Officers are there to help you. It is better to be sure about a rule than to assume. You would never want to lose because you didn't know the rules.

Respect the rules. They are there to make sure that everyone plays the game under the same conditions. Many players do not realize that knowing the rules can help them in many cases.

## Web Sites

- A league's Web site is another great source for information.

- You can access score sheets, rules, and bylaws 24/7.

- When you are not sure of something, you can look it up. Some league sites have a forum for discussion.

- A league Web site may also give you access to your team standings and player stats.

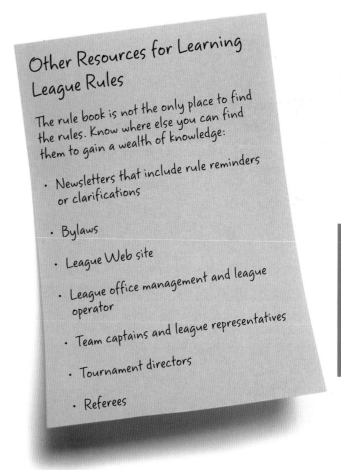

### Other Resources for Learning League Rules

The rule book is not the only place to find the rules. Know where else you can find them to gain a wealth of knowledge:

- Newsletters that include rule reminders or clarifications

- Bylaws

- League Web site

- League office management and league operator

- Team captains and league representatives

- Tournament directors

- Referees

# ETIQUETTE

## Good etiquette will earn you respect from all the teams and players in the league

Etiquette is the best way to show other teams and players just how the game is supposed to be played. Nothing is more enjoyable than playing against a team that is fun to be around and shows good sportsmanship.

Everyone wants to have fun in the league, and everyone wants to win. Competition is the driving force in all of us that

gets our blood flowing. It is good to be competitive, but at the same time you must observe etiquette. No one enjoys a night of pool when someone on the opposing team displays bad manners. When this situation occurs, the captain must step in and talk to the player.

Teams that show good sportsmanship and etiquette rarely

*Sportsmanship*

- Control your temper at all times. Be a good sport. Do not say things to shark your opponent.

- Confirm that a foul has been committed with your opponent before taking ball-in-hand. Don't reach out and grab the cue ball before it stops or scratches.

- Don't break your cue down before the match ends. Shake your opponent's hand before and after the match.

- Have fun! Pool is all about having a good time and an enjoyable night out.

*Waiting Your Turn*

- While your opponent is shooting, stand or sit a reasonable distance from the table.

- Give your opponent a chance to walk away before rushing up there to shoot.

- If another match is going on at the table next to

yours, be aware if anyone else is shooting before you lean down to take a shot.

- Allow a player who is already down on his shot to finish.

have a problem. Most teams react in a positive manner when they see such behavior from the opposing team. If you are on a team that has a player who displays bad sportsmanship, vote that player off the team. Why let your night be ruined because of one player?

When forming a team, let your players know that bad behavior will not be tolerated. If someone gets out of line, you warn him the first time and then drop him from the team the second time. A team has no room for this type of behavior.

## Watching Hits

- When you have a situation in which object balls are close together, ask a third party to watch the hit.

- At higher-level tournaments referees are available to watch close hits.

- A neutral player or referee cannot rule on a hit unless asked to come to the table. The tournament director always has final say.

- When no one is asked, a close call goes to the shooter even when players do not agree, so it's better to be safe than sorry.

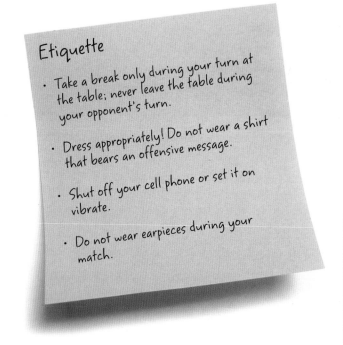

**Etiquette**

- Take a break only during your turn at the table; never leave the table during your opponent's turn.

- Dress appropriately! Do not wear a shirt that bears an offensive message.

- Shut off your cell phone or set it on vibrate.

- Do not wear earpieces during your match.

# LESSONS, EXHIBITIONS & EXPOS

Professional billiard players offer their expertise to help you learn fundamentals and ways to improve your game or for just plain entertainment

### Bruce Barthelette

Bruce can be contacted for events, personal appearances, and trick shot performances. Also, if you have any questions about the trick shots in this book, please contact him. For more information see Bruce's Web site:

www.brucebarthelette.com

### Allison Fisher

Allison can be contacted for individual or group lessons and exhibitions. For more information see Allison's Web site:

www.allisonfisher.com

### Jamey Gray

Jamey can be contacted for trick shot exhibitions. He typically performs exhibitions at pool tournaments, grand openings, youth or senior centers, charitable causes, and for television commercials. For more information see Jamey's Web site:

www.graypool.com

### Gerda Hofstatter

Gerda can be contacted for private or group lessons and exhibitions; she also provides educational exhibitions for corporate events. For more information see Gerda's Web site:

www.gerdahofstatter.com

### Ewa Laurance

Ewa can be contacted for appearances, exhibitions, and business inquiries. For more information see Ewa's Web site:

www.strikingviking.com

### Jeanette Lee

Jeanette can be contacted for appearances and exhibitions. For more information see Jeanette's Web site:

www.jeanettelee.com

### Mike Massey

Mike can be contacted for lessons, personal appearances, and trick shot performances. For more information contact Bruce Barthelette via Web site:

www.brucebarthelette.com or email: ctapa1@aol.com

### Andy Segal

Andy can be contacted for private or corporate parties, exhibitions and trick shot tournaments or events. For more information see Andy's Web site:

www.andysegal.com

## Expos & Trade Shows

### Super Billiards Expo

www.superbilliardsexpo.com
Valley Forge Convention Center
King of Prussia, PA
The Super Billiards Expo is an annual event held in March. This event is where you will find many custom cue exhibitors. Additionally, billiard enthusiasts can find a wide variety of product vendors, meet professional players, and participate in tournament events.

### The Atlanta Billiard Show

www.atlantabilliardshow.com
Phone: (609)226-0646
Email: info@atlantabilliardshow.com
The first annual event for the Atlanta Billiard Show is being held in October 2010 at the Gwinnett Center in Duluth, Georgia. There will be a variety of amateur and professional level tournaments open to players of all ages and also a Trick Shot Tour stop. Custom cue makers and vendors will be on-site displaying products

# POOL LEAGUES & ASSOCIATIONS
The APA is the world's largest amateur league

### American Pool League of Connecticut

P.O. 1290
Enfield, CT 06083-1290
www.ctapa.com
(888) 272-7665

The APA of Connecticut, founded in 1989 by Bruce and Ann Barthelette, is the second largest amateur league in the United States with over 900 teams and 7,000 members. They offer both 8-Ball and 9-Ball Leagues and run local tournaments while using the APA's Equalizer Handicap System. Everyone can play and anyone can win!

### American Poolplayers Association

1000 Lake St. Louis Blvd., Suite 325
Lake St. Louis, MO 63337
www.poolplayers.com
(636) 625-8611

The American Poolplayers Association is the largest amateur pool league in the world with over 270,000 members. It was founded in 1979 by Terry Bell and Larry Hubbart.

### Bruce Barthelette

www.brucebarthelette.com
ctapa1@aol.com
(413) 536-3838

Bruce can be contacted about the APA league in Connecticut and also for questions about the trick shots in this book.

### The Ultimate Trick Shot Tour

www.ultimatetrickshottour.com

The Ultimate Trick Shot Tour, founded in 2009 by Bruce Barthelette, Andy Segal, and Sal Conti, is a series of events featuring top trick shot professionals. Points are accumulated based on tour performance through which players can earn Player of the Year awards and qualifications in *Trick Shot Magic* and the *World Cup of Trick Shots* Championships.

Anyone interested in hosting a professional trick shot artist exhibition, please contact this Web site or call Bruce Barthelette.

### The Women's Professional Billiard Association

www.wpba.com

The WPBA, originally founded in 1976 under the name Women's Professional Billiard Alliance, runs all professional women's tournaments as well as supporting regional tour events. Players accumulate points based on touring performance through which they can earn qualification to participate in other national and world events.

# WHERE TO FIND GEAR

There are many places to find everything you need to play pool including your local billiard halls and billiard supply stores

**Accu-Stats,** www.accu-stats.com
This site has a complete collection of videos on all the pool greats of today and the past.

**Brunswick Billiards,** www.brunswickbilliards.com
Since 1845, Brunswick combines superior craftsmanship, quality, and technology and has been crafting billiard tables. They have a wide selection of tables, light fixtures, accessories, and game room tables.
   Bruce Barthelette would like to thank local Brunswick dealer, Lucchesi Billiards of West Springfield, Massachusetts, for all their help.
   www.lucchesibilliards.com

**Crown Trophy,** www.crowntrophy.com
Crown Trophy, the largest retailer of award and recognition products since its inception in 1978, represents excellent customer service, quality products, and a high level of excellence. They offer trophies, plaques, medals, pins, glass awards, and a selection of other products.

**Cue Stix,** www.cuestixint.com
Cue Stick International, a wholesale billiards supply company, takes pleasure in providing superior customer service, satisfaction guarantee, and fast shipping. They have cues, cases, billiard and game room accessories, and more.

**Delta-13 Racks,** www.delta-13.com
Delta-13 Racks features high quality, consistent tight racks, safe for cloth and designed to create a powerful break preferred by professionals. They offer a lifetime guarantee and also offer Aramith balls and a selection of other billiard products.

**Mueller,** www.poolndarts.com
Mueller, an online billiard and dart supplier, is well known in the industry. They offer an extensive selection of cue sticks, billiard balls, pool tables, dartboards, multiple game room accessories, and more.

**Nick Varner,** www.nickvarner.com
Nick Varner Cues and Cases, a wholesale distributor of billiard supplies since 1999, offers good prices and 100 percent satisfaction guarantee. They offer a variety of accessories, cases, cloth, clothing, specialty items, and cue sticks.

**Ozone Billiards,** www.ozonebilliards.com
   This family-owned and -operated business has a wide selection of pool cues, billiard supplies, and game room products and has a satisfaction guarantee.

**Predator Cues,** www.predatorcues.com
Predator, a leader in the billiards industry since 1994, utilizes innovative technology to manufacture and deliver high quality and performance pool cues. They have a wide selection of cues, shafts, and gear.

**Robin Dodson's Pro Shop,** www.robindodson.com
Robin has a variety of products such as; "Cue-It-Up" cue stick holder, tip tools, jump cues, gloves and more.

**Simonis Cloth,** www.simoniscloth.com
Simonis, making world famous cloth since 1680, is recognized as the industry standard and for producing high quality, professional grade cloth. They have a wide variety of cloth colors in two different fabric blends of wool and nylon.

# ADDITIONAL READING
Here are useful sources to further your game

## Pool and Billiard Magazines
*Billiards Digest*
*Inside Pool*
*Pool & Billiards*
*Professor Q-Balls*

## Pool and Billiard Books
*The Best Damn Pool Instruction Book Period!* by Ron Schneider. Frederick Fell Publishers, 2005

*The Black Widow's Guide to Killer Pool: Become the Player to Beat* by Jeanette Lee and Adam Scott Gershenson. Three Rivers Press, 2000

*Byrne's New Standard Book of Pool and Billiards* by Robert Byrne. Mariner Books. 1998

*Capelle's Practicing Pool* by Phil Capelle. Billiards Press, 2006

*The Ewa Mataya Pool Guide* by Ewa Mataya with Bob Brown. Harper Perennial, 1995

*Mike Massey's World of Trick Shots* by Phil Capelle and Mike Massey. Billiards Press, 2003

*A Mind for Pool: How to Master the Mental Game* by Philip B. Capelle. Billards Press, 1999

*The 99 Critical Shots in Pool: Everything You Need to Know to Learn and Master the Game* by Ray "Cool Cat" Martin and Rosser Reeves. Random House Puzzles & Games, 1993

*Play Your Best Pool: Secrets to Winning 8-Ball & 9-Ball* by Philip B. Capelle. Billiards Press, 2005

*Pleasures of Small Motions: Mastering the Mental Game of Pocket Billiards* by Bob Fancher, Ph.D. The Lyons Press, 2002

*Precision Pool* by Gerry Kanov and Shari Stauch. Human Kinetics, 2007

# GLOSSARY

Learn the language of the game and become a more knowledgeable player

**7-Ball:** A contemporary rotation pool game with rules similar to 9-ball that involves shooting balls numbered 1 through 7 in order and in specified pockets. One of the players selects three pockets for the other player before the game starts. The player who chose the pockets shoots in the opposite three pockets.

**8-Ball:** A game which involves shooting at a category of ball (either stripes or solids) and pocketing all of them before shooting in the game-winning 8 ball.

**9-Ball:** A game which involves shooting in rotation from the lowest numbered ball to the highest (1 through 9). The game-winning ball is the 9 ball.

**10-Ball:** A rotation pool game very similar to 9-Ball but more difficult, which involves shooting balls numbered 1 through 10 in order instead of nine balls. In this game, the 10 ball is the game winning ball instead of the 9 ball.

**Ball-in-Hand:** *Ball-in-Hand* refers to the reward given to your opponent when you foul or scratch. Your opponent may place the cue ball anywhere on the table.

**Bank Pool:** A pool game that players score by banking called balls off a cushion into a called pocket.

**Bank Shot:** A *bank shot* is when a player hits an object ball into a rail or multiple rails first before pocketing it.

**Bar Box Table:** Slang term used to refer to the smaller 3½ foot by 7 foot size table. This size is most commonly found in bars and is coin operated.

**Bed:** The playing surface of the table.

**Behind the Line:** A ball located in the area between the head strin and head rail.

**Billiard Trade Show:** A *Billiard Trade Show* is an event you ca attend that will have a variety of cue stick makers, product vendo and tournaments.

**Blocker Ball:** A ball that is in the way of a clean hit to your object ba

**Bowliards:** *Bowliards* is a pool game often used as a practice dr The game uses a scoring method similar to ten-pin bowling in whic a player shoots ten racks of ten balls, comparable to frames ar bowling pins. Each player gets a maximum of two innings to pock the ten balls in each of the racks.

**Break (Break Shot):** This is the opening shot of the game.

**Break and Run Player:** A player who breaks and runs out all th balls on a regular basis.

**Break Cue:** An alternate cue used for breaking that usually has a ve hard tip on it.

**Breakout Ball:** A *breakout ball* is an object ball a shooter will pock or shoot off of that will get the cue ball to break apart a cluster of ball

**Breakout Shot:** A *breakout shot* is when the shooter breaks out cluster of balls by shooting into or off another object ball.

**Bridge:** This refers to the hand that holds and guides the cue sti and how you hold the cue stick or the type of hold used e.g., ope closed (Hand Bridge). This term also refers to a stick with a plate c the end that is shaped to hold and guide the cue stick when th shooter can't reach the spot where he would normally place h bridge hand (Mechanical Bridge).

232

**Called Ball:** The target object ball you intend to sink in a called pocket.

**Called Pocket:** A pocket you designate and tell your opponent you will shoot the shot into.

**Called Safety:** A *called safety* is when you have no intention of pocketing a ball and you announce that you are playing a safety or defensive shot.

**Carom Shot:** A *carom shot* is when you skim one object ball off another object ball to go toward a pocket.

**Chalk:** A small cube of dry, powder, adhesive, colored substance that is applied to the tip of the cue stick regularly. The most commonly used chalk color is blue.

**Close the Angle:** When the cue ball rebounds off the cushion at a greater angle than the angle of approach.

**Cluster:** A group of object balls that are very close together or touching each other.

**Combination Shot:** This is when a player shoots the cue ball into one object ball to pocket another object ball. Two ball combinations are the most common; however, combinations with more than two balls are also possible but much more difficult.

**Contact Point:** The spot on the object ball that the cue ball must hit in order to pocket the ball.

**Cross Bank Shot:** When the cue ball crosses the path of the object ball before it goes in the pocket.

**Cross Corner:** A bank shot into the opposite corner pocket.

**Cross Side:** A bank shot into the opposite side pocket.

**Cue Ball:** The all-white ball (sometimes with red spots) you shoot at with a cue stick, this ball needs be contacted first in order to pocket an object ball.

**Cue Stick Extender:** This is a hard plastic device used to attach on the butt end of a cue stick and make the stick longer for hitting a ball that is out of reach.

**Curve:** The reaction of the cue ball off an object ball or rail when you apply English to it.

**Cushion (also see Rail):** The raised surface surrounding the edge of the bed or playing area of the table.

**Cut Bank Shot:** A bank shot which you must also cut in order to bank the ball in a pocket. The cut causes transference of English to the object ball. The object ball English can be negated by applying English to the cue ball that is on the same side as the cut.

**Cut Shot:** Any shot that has an angle on it.

**Dead-in:** A term used to describe when a shot is in direct line to a pocket with a center cue ball hit. For example; a dead-in combination would mean both balls are in a straight line to the pocket and a dead-in bank would mean if you hit the object ball direct (100 percent of the ball) it will travel on an angle that leads straight into a pocket.

**Defensive Shot:** A *defensive shot* is when a shooter deliberately misses his ball in order to pass up his turn to an opponent. Playing defense is perfectly legal and a good strategy.

**Deflection:** *Deflection* refers to the path of the cue ball when right or left English is applied to it.

**Diamonds:** The markings along the rails on a table that can be used as visual reference throughout the course of a game. They can be used to calculate banks or kicks and target position routes.

**Diamond System:** A method used for bank and kick shots that involves mathematical calculations of the angles using the diamond markings along the rail.

**Double Elimination:** A tournament format in which you are eliminated after you lose twice.

**Draw:** A way of stroking the cue ball to get the cue ball to come back toward you after contacting an object ball. The cue's tip must contact the cue ball below center to apply backspin in order for draw to work.

**Duck:** An easy shot, hanging in or very close to a pocket.

**Elevated Bridge:** Raising the palm of the bridge hand up off the table in order to shoot over another ball that is too close to the cue ball.

**End Rail:** This refers to either the head rail or the foot rail.

**English:** An application of side spin by contacting either side of the center cue ball axis with the tip of your cue stick. English causes the cue ball to curve left or right after contact with an object ball or rail.

**Exhibition:** A public show or display of talent such as those professionals perform in pocket billiards or artistic pool (trick shots) or a display of product such as latest trends and innovations from the billiard world for professionals and hobbyists.

**Ferrule:** The hard piece of plastic or ivory at the end of the stick where the tip is attached.

**Follow:** Stroking the cue ball to make it travel in the same direction as the object ball after contact. The cue's tip must hit the cue ball above center in order to follow.

**Follow Through:** This is an important and desirable motion of the cue stick carrying through the area previously occupied by the cue ball.

**Foot Spot:** A spot placed in the exact center of an imaginary line drawn across the foot side of the pool table between the second diamonds up from the foot rail. The foot side of the table is where balls are racked, or on the same side as the ball return on tables that have them.

**Foul:** An illegal shot resulting in loss of turn at the table for the shooter and cue ball in-hand for the opponent. There are seven ways a player can foul such as accidentally moving or touching the cue ball, double hitting the cue ball, missing an object ball completely, scratching the cue ball in a pocket or flying it off the table and contacting an object ball but no ball hits a rail afterward.

**Frozen (Ball to Ball/Ball to Rail):** A frozen ball is a ball that is touching either another ball or a rail and as such is considered frozen to another ball or frozen on the rail.

**Full Ball:** When the cue ball hits the object ball straight on or 100 percent.

**Full Hit:** When the cue ball needs to contact more of the object ball (closer to a full ball or 100 percent) in order to make a shot.

**Game:** A single rack played between two players. In league play the number of games a player needs to win is determined by the skill levels of the two players competing. In recreational play and when playing with more than one other person, you complete one rack or game; then the next person will rotate in to play the next game against the winner of the game that just finished.

**Ghost Ball:** An imaginary cue ball you visualize next to the object ball in order to determine the spot the cue ball needs to hit the object ball. This is a method used to help a player aim.

**Good Hit:** When the cue ball hits the intended object ball prior to anything else.

**Half Ball:** When the cue ball hits 50 percent of the object ball.

**Hanger:** When a ball is sitting in the jaws of the pocket near the edge.

**Head Rail:** The rail between the two corner pockets from the side the table you break from.

**Head String:** The imaginary line drawn across the head side of the pool table between the second diamonds up from the head rail. The head of the table is where a player lags or breaks from, or on the end opposite the ball return on tables that have them.

**Hit (the):** The feel of using a particular cue stick.

**Hooked:** When an object ball you need to hit is blocked by another object ball sitting in the direct path of the cue ball.

**House Stick:** An inexpensive one piece cue owned by bar or billiard hall owners who provide this stick for patrons to use.

**In Line:** Putting the cue ball in a good position for the next shot.

**Inning:** An inning is a player's turn at the table. When you are playing against an opponent or in league play, an inning occurs when the player who loses the lag (or second shooter) completes his turn at the table. An inning does not count when the rack is over (e.g. when the player sinks the 8 ball earning the break for the next rack or with the game-winning shot.)

**Inside English:** Applying side spin on the cue ball that is the same side as the direction of the cut.

**Intentional Foul:** A strategy in which a player purposely gives his opponent ball-in-hand.

**Jack Up:** Raising the bridge hand up in order to shoot over another ball that is too close to the cue ball or when a shot is on or near a rail.

**Jaws:** The area of the playing surface that is inside the edge of the pocket.

**Joint:** The connecting piece of the cue in the middle where the shaft meets the butt.

**Jump Cue:** A specialty cue made specifically for jump shots. These cues normally have harder tips, are shorter and lighter than a normal playing cue.

**Jump Over:** When the shooter executes a jump shot and clears a blocking object ball.

**Jump Shot:** A *jump shot* is when the cue ball is struck in a downward fashion for the purpose of flying the cue ball over a blocker object ball in order to achieve a legal hit. It is a foul to execute a jump shot by scooping the cue ball. Although jump shots are legal in league and tournament play, house rules will prevail. Remember to always double check with establishment owners if jump shots are permissible.

**Kick Shot:** A *kick shot* is when a player shoots the cue ball into the rail or multiple rails first before contacting an object ball.

**Kiss:** When the object ball ricochets off another ball or when the object ball kicks back and hits the cue ball after being contacted by it (aka double kiss.)

**Kitchen:** The area of the table between the head string and head rail.

**Lag (for the Break):** A method used to start off a match. Players simultaneously shoot a ball from behind the head string, bank it off the foot rail and back to the head of the table. The ball that comes closest to the head rail without touching the side rails or going in a pocket wins the lag and that player gets to break the first rack. The balls may hit the head rail. If the balls hit a side rail or go in a pocket, that player loses the lag. If the balls touch, players need to re-lag.

**Lag Shot:** A very soft stroke used to either pocket a ball or start off the match.

**Lathe:** This is a machine or equipment used by professional cue makers for maintaining wraps, ferrules, shafts, and tips on cue sticks.

**Leave:** A term used to describe when your cue ball has landed in a good position for taking your next shot.

**Long (bank shot that goes long):** A bank shot that misses on the far side of the pocket. When an object ball or the cue ball goes past the spot you intend for it to land.

**Long Center Line:** An imaginary line that runs through the center of the table from the head rail to the foot rail. When balls are spotted, they are placed along the Long Center Line beginning with the foot spot. If the foot spot is occupied, balls are then spotted and frozen to other object balls along the same line going toward the foot rail.

**Long Rail:** The rail that is the entire length of the table.

**Long Rail Bank:** A bank shot that goes the entire length of the table.

**Marked Pocket (also see Called Pocket):** A designated pocket for the 8 ball that you place an object next to in order to tell your opponent where you are shooting it. It is recommended you do not use chalk to mark the pocket.

**Massé Cue:** A specialty cue made specifically for massé shots. These cues are normally the heaviest ones made and can be up to the maximum legal weight of 25 ounces.

**Massé Shot:** When the cue ball curves as a result of spin applied to the cue ball with an elevated cue.

**Match:** A competition between two players, in league or tournament play. .

**Matching Up:** A negotiation preceding a match. In league play, captains decide which one of their players will play against the other team's player.

**Miscue:** A *miscue* occurs when the cue stick's tip does not hit enough of the cue ball and skims off it without sending the cue ball along the intended path. A miscue can result from not using enough chalk, trying to use too much English, or from an improperly shaped tip. A miscue may sometimes result in a foul; however, the miscue itself is not a foul unless the shooter deliberately miscues to scoop over another ball.

**Miss:** When you are trying for a shot and the ball does not go in a pocket.

**Mushrooming (Tip):** When the tip of your cue stick becomes flattened out or wider than its original shape.

**Natural Angle:** The path the cue ball will travel after contacting an object ball or a rail, without the effect of friction.

**Normal (Regular) Playing Cue:** This is the cue stick used by a player for the majority of shots that he takes in a match.

**Object Ball:** A striped or solid ball that is your targeted ball for a shot or any other ball in your category.

**One Piece Cue:** A cue stick that comes in one piece and cannot be broken down. These are the least expensive kind and are most commonly used as house sticks.

**One-quarter Ball Hit:** When the cue ball hits 25 percent of the object ball.

**On the Break:** Making the game winning ball (8 or 9) on the break shot.

**Open Bridge:** A hand bridge formed by making a *v* between your thumb and index finger in order to hold and guide the cue stick.

**Opening Break:** The very first shot of a match (the break).

**Outside English:** Applying side spin on the cue ball that is on the opposite side than on the direction of the cut.

**Pattern Play:** Shooting the balls in a specific order and/or a particular style of position play.

**Pill Pool:** A rotation pool game played by first drawing numbered marker balls (also called peas or pills) from a shaker bottle before starting. Players then take turns shooting the balls in numerical order from 1 through 15 until they miss or pocket their own number.

**Pinch:** The type of stroke used when trapping the cue ball between the tip and the slate.

**Player:** A person who plays very well, especially when in competition.

**Pocket Billiards:** This is the formal name for the game of pool.

**Pocket Point:** The sharp edge where the pocket and the rail meet.

**Position Area (also see Target Zone):** An area on the table where the cue ball needs to land in order to be in place for a makeable next shot. It is a good idea to visualize a good size area in case the position play is not exact.

**Problem Ball:** An object ball that is sitting in a position with no clear path to a pocket or is blocked by other balls. A problem ball prevents a player from having an easy run out.

**Professional Player:** A player who makes a living by playing and through their involvement in the sport.

**Punch Stroke:** A quick rigid stroke with a short follow-through.

**Push Out:** A strategy that can be used immediately after the break by a breaker when a ball is pocketed on the break or by an incoming player when no balls are pocketed on the break. A push out can be elected when a player does not want to take the shot he is faced with. This strategy involves telling the opponent you plan to push out then shooting the cue ball to another position without having to make a legal hit. The incoming player can then choose to take the shot from the new position or pass it back. Standard game rules apply from that point on.

**Push Shot:** A *push shot* involves a situation where the cue ball is frozen to the object ball. Push shots are controversial and are often not called as fouls. Decrease your chances of being accused of shooting a push shot by elevating the butt of your cue 30 degrees or shooting the cue ball into the object ball on an angle.

**Race:** The amount of points or games a player needs to win. The winner of a match is determined by whoever is the first player to reach their number (e.g. race to 150 points or race to 5 games.)

**Rack:** Triangular or diamond shaped tool used to set the balls in place before a game starts or the layout of the balls after the rack has been removed.

**Rail (also see Cushion):** The raised surface surrounding the edge of the bed or playing area of the table. This includes the cushions.

**Rail Bridge:** A hand bridge formed by placing the hand on the rail.

**Rail Shot:** When the cue ball is frozen on or very close to the rail.

**Regulation Size Table:** A table is considered a Regulation Size Table when it is 4½ feet x 9 feet in size or any table where the length is twice the width.

**Reverse English:** Application of side spin on the cue ball that causes it to come off the cushion in a sharper angle than when it went into the cushion.

**Rotation Game:** A game which involves using all fifteen balls and shooting them in order from the lowest numbered ball to the highest (1 through 15 balls).

**Run:** The number of balls a player makes in one turn.

**Run Out:** When a number of balls are made in succession up to and including the game-winning ball.

**Running English:** Application of English that opens up the angle off a cushion and also makes the cue ball move faster after contacting the cushion.

**Safe/Safety:** A strategy in which a player does not intend to pocket a ball in an attempt to keep his opponent from making a shot or to leave him with a tough shot.

**Score:** The number of points or games a player has at any time during the match.

**Scratch:** When the cue ball falls in one of the pockets.

**Scratch Shot:** A shot where there is a high probability of scratching or a scratch is unable to be avoided.

**Sell Out:** When you take a low percentage shot because there's no good opportunity for a defense, even though you realize going for this shot will cost you the game if you miss.

**Shape (also see Position Area):** Where the cue ball lands for the next shot after making a shot.

**Shark:** When a player tries to distract or throw off the shooter.

**Short:** A bank shot that misses on the near side of the pocket. When an object ball or the cue ball stops before reaching the spot where you intend for it to land.

**Short Rail:** The rail that is the entire width of the table.

**Short Rail Bank:** A bank shot across the width of the table.

**Side Rail (also see Long Rail):** The rail that runs along the length of the table.

**Single Elimination:** A tournament format in which you are eliminated after you lose once.

**Slate:** The hard playing surface the bed of the table is made up of. This is the surface that is below the cloth.

**Snooker:** A pool game played on a large table 12 feet x 6 feet with six pockets. Snooker is played using a white cue ball and different colored Snooker balls approximately 2¼ inches in diameter. There are fifteen red balls and one yellow, green, brown, blue, pink, and black ball. Each ball is worth a number of points. The player (or team) scoring the most points, using the cue ball to pot the red and colored balls, wins.

**Soft Break:** When a player breaks the balls just hard enough for the legal number (four object balls in the games of 8-Ball and 9-Ball) of balls to hit a rail.

**Speed:** How hard or soft of a stroke used to hit the ball. This can sometimes be related to a scale of 1 through 10 with 1 being the softest and 10 being the hardest.

**Speed Control:** Controlling the cue ball's rolling distance. Good speed control is the key to playing good position.

**Speed Pool:** A pool game which involves shooting all the balls on the table in any order as fast as possible. A stopwatch is used to time games. If competing against others, each player shoots an entire rack (or game) and the player who does it with the fastest time wins.

**Spot:** A location on the table such as the foot spot where balls are spotted. Also refers to re-placing a ball on the table such as an object ball that flies off the table or the game winning 9 ball (in 9-Ball) if it is pocketed while a foul is committed.

**Squirt (also see Deflection):** Changing the path of the cue ball by applying right or left English to it.

**Stance:** The position of your body when you take a shot.

**Stitch Safety:** A *stitch safety* is when the cue ball lies behind a ball that does not allow a direct to an object ball.

**Stop Shot:** A *stop shot* is when you hit the cue ball directly in the center in order to stop the cue ball dead once it contacts the object ball. This works best when shooting a ball straight on, full or when contacting 100 percent of it.

**Straight in Shot:** This is when the cue ball and object ball are lined up in a straight line to the pocket.

**Straight Pool:** A game also known as 14.1 in which each player races to a certain number of points. Each time a ball is pocketed in a called pocket, a point is scored.

**Stroke:** Movement of the arm, wrist, and hand that makes the cue stick shoot through the cue ball.

**Table Scratch/Table Foul:** When you create a foul without the cue ball going in one of the six pockets. A table foul occurs when you miss a ball completely, disturb the cue ball, or when no ball hits a rail after making contact with an intended object ball.

**Table Speed:** The natural roll of the cue ball across the table.

**Tangent Line:** The path the ball takes after making contact with another ball. This is usually at a 90 degree angle where the edge of the ball will travel along.

**Target Zone (also see Position Area):** An area on the table where the cue ball needs to land in order to be in place for a makeable next shot. It is a good idea to visualize a good size area in case the position play is not exact.

**Thin Cut (Thinner):** When the cue ball needs to contact only a small part of the object ball (ninety degrees or 25 percent) in order to make a shot.

**Three-quarter Ball Hit:** When the cue ball hits 75 percent of the object ball.

**Three Rail Bank:** A bank shot in which the object ball contacts three rails before it goes into a pocket.

**Three Rail Kick:** A kick shot in which the cue ball contacts three rails prior to hitting an object ball.

**Throw:** When you change cut angle of an object ball as a result of friction between balls. Both English and contact can cause throw. Apply the opposite English from the direction you wish to cut the ball (e.g., apply Left English on the cue ball to throw the object ball to the right.) When multiple balls are involved, throw affects all the balls involved in the shot.

**Timeout:** Used in league play. A *Timeout* is when a shooter is playing a league match and asks for advice from another team member (coach) about their shot (e.g., which shot to take or how to shoot it). Asking a question about a rule is not considered a timeout.

**Tip:** A small rounded leather piece of material attached to the ferrule at the end of a cue stick's shaft. Tips are made in different hardness (soft, medium, hard) and also made layered or unlayered. Tip also refers to a way of describing application of English (e.g. use ½ tip to 1 tip of English on the cue ball.)

**Trick Shot:** A special shot played on a pool table that does unusual things with the balls that would seem unlikely. Props are often used as part of a shot, and the balls are set up in ways they may or may not appear during normal game play.

**Trick Shot Artist:** A professional or amateur player who is known mostly for his or her trick shot skills. These players may enter professional trick shot competitions, may be known entertainers who perform trick shot exhibitions, or may be professional pool players who perform trick shots on the side as another profession. This does not include players who do trick shots but are not known for performing or entering competitions with them.

**Two Piece Cue:** A cue that has a joint in the middle to connect the shaft with the butt end of the cue stick.

**Two Rail Bank:** A bank shot in which the object ball contacts two rails before it goes into a pocket.

**Two Rail Kick:** A kick shot in which the cue ball contacts two rails prior to hitting an object ball.

**Two Way Shot:** A lower percentage shot that will leave you in a good position for your next shot and leave your opponent with a tougher shot in case you miss. Going for a shot and playing safe at the same time.

**Wing Balls:** The two balls that are on either side of a 9-Ball rack.

**Wrap:** Some cues will have this over the wood on the butt end where you grip the cue stick with your back hand. Wraps can be made of leather, Irish linen, or cork. Irish linen is the most commonly used wrap.

# INDEX

INDEX

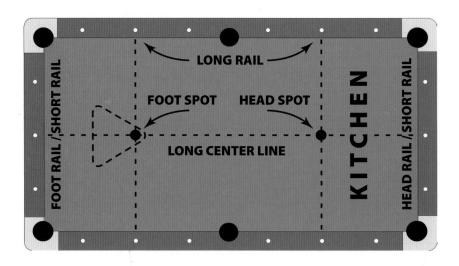